No Boxing Allowed

Nola Anne Hennessy

Copyright © 2009, 2012, 2013, 2016 by Nola Anne Hennessy

All rights reserved. No part of this book may be used or reproduced by any means graphic, electronic, or mechanical, including photocopying, recording, taping or by any information storage retrieval system without the written permission of the publisher and author, except in the case of brief quotations which may be embodied in critical articles and reviews with due reference to the source.

This book may be ordered through booksellers or by contacting the publisher:

Serenidad Consulting Pty Ltd
PO Box 881
Sanctuary Cove QLD 4212
Australia

Ph: +61 7 55148077
Fax: +61 7 55148088
Email: enquiry@serenidadconsulting.com
www.serenidadconsulting.com

ISBN: 978-0-9874599-0-9 (sc)
ISBN: 978-0-9874599-1-6 (hc)
ISBN: 978-0-9874599-2-3 (e)

US Library of Congress Control Number: 2012904150

Australian National Library CIP - Dewey Number: 158.1

The views expressed in this work are solely those of the author. The author does not dispense medical advice or prescribe the use of any technique as a form of treatment for a physical, emotional or mental condition and advises that a qualified physician must be consulted by the reader under those circumstances. The intent of the author is only to offer information of a general nature to help you in your quest for holistic well-being, self awareness, and improved relationships in every context. In the event you use any of the information in this book for yourself, which is your constitutional and/or legal right, the author and the publisher assume no responsibility for your actions.

Cover by Fineline Advertising, New Jersey USA

Front cover image is based on a photograph taken by Kevin Jones

Serenidad Consulting Pty Ltd - revision date 9/15/2016

CONTENTS

Dedication..iii
Author's Special Note v
Foreword..vii
Introduction..ix

PART 1: THE JOURNEY TO SELF-REALIZATION

Chapter 1: Beyond Self-Actualization 3
Chapter 2: What is Personal Power? 5
Chapter 3: What is Positional Power? 15
Chapter 4: Self-Exploration - Recognizing Where You Are At....23
Chapter 5: What Do I Need and Want? 39
Chapter 6: Internal Programming 43
Chapter 7: Mixed Messages and Mind Games.............................54
Chapter 8: Growing Beyond Fear 60
Chapter 9: Letting Go Of The Baggage 66
Chapter 10: Using Personal Power to Re-engineer Your
            Thinking and Re-program Your Mind
            To The Positive 74

PART 2: THE CONSTRUCTIVE USE OF PERSONAL POWER

Chapter 1: Positive and Negative Applications of Power 82
Chapter 2: The Virtues of Great Leadership.................................90
Chapter 3: Leaders: Born or Made? 95
Chapter 4: Realizing Your Full Potential 99

PART 3: ACHIEVING A LASTING AND POSITIVE IMPACT

Chapter 1:	Eliminating Presentism 105
Chapter 2:	Building Successful Business Partnerships...................109
Chapter 3:	Using Power Effectively in Command and Control (C2) Organizations 114
Chapter 4:	Enriching Personal Relationships................................120
Chapter 5:	Priceless Gifts 124

DEDICATION

This book is dedicated to the following special people:

Son Nick, especially, for his time, love, humor, patience, advice, warmth, devotion and understanding. Nick has been a true friend as well as a fine son. His willingness to share and discuss his views on world events and cultural changes, has injected a special meaning to my life that I wouldn't have experienced had I not become a mother. I admire his courage, strength under the worst adversity, generosity, persistence to achieve his goals, and honesty. I believe I have the finest son ever born.

To those who repeatedly encouraged me to write, enquired about the book's progress and waited very patiently for its unveiling.

And to Shirley MacLaine, for "Don't Fall Off The Mountain"[1] and "You Can Get There From Here"[2].

From the depths of my soul, thank you.

---

[1] Bantam Books & W.W. Norton & Company Inc, ©Shirley MacLaine 1970

[2] Corgi Books, ©Shirley MacLaine 1975

AUTHOR'S SPECIAL NOTE

Over many decades I have observed relationships, behaviors and the impact of people's choices. In the last decade alone, since my first manuscript was completed, many changes have occurred in our world.

In late 2008 I reflected on the incoming President of the United States of America and his intentions whilst in office. His impact on the world was destined to be noticeable, if not profound. In November 2008 we heard the President-elect say "those who seek peace and stability — we support you".

That President is being replaced soon, however the peace and stability he spoke of are even more relevant today. Our world is unpredictable and humans, quite rightly, will always function better in a world that has some semblance of stability and calm. All leaders, and those who grow to become Great Leaders, will need to remain focused on peace, stability, integrity and compassion, for without them we are likely to invoke our own extinction.

To every reader of this book, remember that when an individual, group, community, nation or group of nations step forward to make things better, huge resistance can be placed in front of us. My recommendation to you, as an important contributor in that journey, is that you stay strong, hold faith, and hold the light for positive change, and goodness and peace will become our outcome. Peace and a return to embraced goodness is what humanity needs to achieve, in order to ensure its survival. The system of universal justice will always support your positive efforts.

Your friend in peace,

Ada

September 15, 2016

FOREWORD

(an excerpt thereof, dated June 2007)

For many, life is a search for some level of understanding that might help explain the world to themselves. But Nola is more than just an observer, more than a 'watcher of the skies'. While the patterns try hard to protect themselves, Nola has found them and offered these patterns to us here.

There is a rich range of ideas, suggestions and lessons in this book, but I especially enjoyed Nola's thoughts on leadership. Her discussion centers on leadership behavior and is one of the most valuable checklists I have seen.

Nola is, in this book, a teacher. This is her gift to us. She has offered a way for us to avoid being boxed in by the habits, behavior and expectations of the people that surround us. I congratulate Nola for showing us the things she believes in.

Extract from 'Say Not The Struggle Naught Availeth', a poem by Arthur Hugh Clough:
For while the tired waves, vainly breaking, Seem
*   here no painful inch to gain,*
Far back through creeks and inlets making
*   Comes silent, flooding in, the main.*
And not by eastern windows only,
*   When daylight comes, comes in the light, In*
front the sun climbs slow, how slowly,
*   But westward, look, the land is bright.*

Ian Gordon
Major General (Rtd)
Australian Army

INTRODUCTION

For my entire professional career, which started in 1973 with my first senior management position, I have been intrigued and inspired by human behaviour, people's attitudes and their choices. Societies and their people have changed significantly over the decades since the 1950's, when I was born. Now, people appear to want more, spend more, take more, talk more, use more, discard more, waste more, punish more, demand more and ignore more. But do they give or listen or nurture or empathize or discern or help more?

Whether you are running your own enterprise, employed by someone else, are the Chief Executive of an organization, embarking on your first career, managing a small team, studying to achieve a higher level of understanding, stepping into your first supervisory role, parenting a child, or simply engaging in a relationship with friends and family, you have something to gain from reading this book.

In No Boxing Allowed I articulate the value of allowing yourself to reach your full potential, without restrictions and limitations; without being suffocated by, nor suffocating others with, controlling behavior, confusion, apathy, selfishness, hidden agendas, lies and deceit. My words are expected to encourage you to forge beyond the boundaries and labels that others attempt to impose on you and you impose on yourself.

My teachings will challenge your emotions, beliefs, opinions and attitudes. I will help you to identify personal power within yourself and, I trust, make you think about or re-evaluate why you are here on Earth; what you offer; what good you can do in making the world a better place; and how you can help others.

I do have one wish, as you read. That you find courage — courage to: always believe in yourself, face and erase fears, think outside the box, challenge your own negative thinking and that of others, and step forward into uncertainty with a brave and open heart. I hope that you find courage to determine new ways to meet life's needs, be more self-reliant, be realistic in your expectations of yourself and others, and have courage to ask for help. And that you find courage to take full and complete control of yourself, and not seek to control others[3].

I hope you can trust in yourself that what you have to offer and what you can contribute to life, and to this world, will bring positive, lasting results, not just for you but for others.

Everything is exactly as it should be, right now, right in this space. Dreams are being born. You are being awakened to a whole new way of life and whether you consciously work to make the changes happen or not, they will happen anyway.

FIND COURAGE and TRUST THE JOURNEY

---

[3] The only exceptions to this being those people to whom their care and safety is entrusted to you — children and the ill or infirmed

PART 1

The Journey to Self-Realization

CHAPTER 1
Beyond Self-Actualization

Abraham Maslow[4] first introduced the concept of a Hierarchy of Needs to describe the human state of awareness — Physiological and Safety Needs, Belongingness and Love Needs, Esteem Needs and Self-Actualization Needs. The need state of Self-Actualization was deemed to be achieved when all other needs had been satisfied and was a measure of true self-fulfilment.

Self-Actualizer's were described as possessing many qualities including the ability to judge objectively, see reality, be non-conformist, democratic and fair, be self-reliant and comfortable being alone, accepting others as they are and having the capacity to realize deep relationships with a few close and intimate friends, rather than many superficial relationships.

Interestingly, my opinion is that Maslow's state of Self-Actualization was restrictive in its own right. It boxed people into a certain category — acting this way, thinking that way, allowing certain relationship scenarios, and so on.

Over time, others have adapted Maslow's hierarchy to accommodate other need structures, including Transcendence Needs i.e. the point where humans help others to achieve Self-Actualization. I agree, there is certainly value in being able to describe the point at which you have reached the ability to help others. Helping others to win in life is a positive use of personal power. But, isn't the state of Transcendence still a label, a boundary?

---

[4] Dr Abraham Harold Maslow, 1908-1970, Doctor of Psychology

The term self-realization is noted in tens of thousands of contexts, most often in relation to religion or spirituality. In the context of my teachings in this book however, self-realization is not about finding God, or describing or labelling yourself a certain way e.g. a Self-Realizer. It is a time of awakening, where you really recognize and tap into your true essence, understand why you are here on Earth, and what your higher level purpose is in life; and understand that in order to give goodness to the world for the benefit of the many, selflessness must prevail and great courage must be drawn from within.

The ability to journey to self-realization is within everyone, in each lifetime. The willingness, motivation, determination and self-control necessary to get there however, is purely dependent on your personal choice.

You are about to embark on a journey of self-discovery and empowerment. This is a new beginning for you, so relax and open your mind. Allow my teachings to enter in your conscious mind and the subconscious to process the information the way it knows best, overnight and over time. Rest assured, the information you need for your survival and happiness will be retained, and will act as a solid foundation into the future. And, at any time in the future, you can reflect back, using even the brief statements highlighted throughout the text as your guide, to reprogram your subconscious with positive, empowering thoughts.

The messages and teachings in this book are enduring. There is no expiry date for what I teach because my teachings are based on the fundamentals of goodness, honesty and integrity, coupled with the values and morals that humanity is crying out to embrace again.

CHAPTER 2

What is Personal Power?

Power is, according to the Encarta Dictionary, "the ability, skill or capacity to do something". When we think of *personal power* however, it is more about that innate strength that lies within each human being — strength of mind, strength of heart, strength of soul. Personal power is any and all of the following:
- the inner power you feel when positive or negative emotions are heightened;
- the atmosphere, sensation or impression you radiate;
- your ability to influence the judgment and emotions of others — your persuasiveness; and
- not dependent on positional power to have effect.

Personal power is yours and yours alone. It can be used to the benefit or detriment of both yourself and others, by your choice. Identifying the personal power that you possess, harnessing it (i.e. by strong self-control) and then learning to give and channel it in positive, constructive ways takes time, practice and commitment.

Every day we see examples of the misuse of personal power — violence in the streets, the assault of a human being, graffiti, vandalism, intimidation and bullying of others, refusing to listen to someone speak, the denial of words previously spoken, and the scorn or ridicule of a loved one.

As humans beings we live on earth surrounded by energies of varying influence. In our own right we are electromagnetic beings, influenced by the position of our planet in relation to others in the universe. Energy runs through us all the time.

By the very force of gravity we are held on earth. The power that the universe has over us as humans on the earth, is both simple and profound. Can we choose to step off planet earth and find somewhere else to live? Yes, but only in a space craft that is capable of producing enough power against gravitational forces to project us into space and carry us to our destination.

Our destination must also be suitable to sustain life. Can we fly 30,000 feet above the earth? Yes, but only in an aircraft and with equipment that provides the necessary environment for us to survive at that height.

For centuries humans have been healing themselves and each other energetically. The terms Chi, Qi, karma, aura and Reiki are terms more widely recognized now than ever before. And while scientists are still researching the existence of bodily energy, and its pathways or meridians, we humans are out there delivering our energy to the universe, every second, even while we sleep.

What is most obvious to me and profound for the human race, is that very few humans realize that the energy they put out into the universe is far more important, in the strategic impact sense, than anything else they do. Your use of personal power and the choices you make every day are far more important than whether you have loads of money in the bank, what type of car you drive, what size home you live in, what label clothes you wear. Your next ego boost, whilst undoubtedly giving you instant gratification, is not at all important in the bigger picture for humanity.

So what is that inner energy or power that we all have inside? Let's look at the two examples—firstly *negative energy* and secondly, but most importantly, *positive energy*.

Negative energy is always there — you can choose to hold it inside, project it out or erase it for good. As youngsters most of you would have been subjected to bullying or victimization by a sibling or at school by your "friends". Even as adults you are likely to have been subjected to this treatment at work by a co-worker, member of staff or a manager at one time or another; or even in your closest personal relationships with loved ones. If you are one of the rare people who didn't receive such treatment, you are truly fortunate.

Let's look at that aspect more closely and, for those who experienced another's negative impact, let's revisit that experience to enhance your understanding of your own inner energy.

NB. You may wish to have another person talk you through these memory recall exercises, so that you can properly focus on the doing, rather than the actual text. Either way, the words should be read or spoken with calmness, in a slower and more gentle tone than you would normally speak. Take some deep breaths, center yourself, clear you mind and then proceed:

(Negative energy — Exercise One) "Take a minute to get comfortable and relaxed, make sure your head is supported and your arms and legs are uncrossed. (Pause) Close your eyes. (Pause) Now remember back to a time when you were upset — remember how you felt deep inside. (Long Pause)

Keep focused on the feeling; center it in your solar plexus, near your stomach. (Pause) Don't waver from the feeling. (Pause) Let it grow in intensity, feel the heat, and feel the power building up . . . . spend a few minutes remembering. (Pause for 2-3 minutes)

As soon as you are ready to stop remembering, then *stop*, instantly. (Pause). Now, take some time to let your body return to a feeling of equilibrium and happiness. (Pause) Take some deep breaths and *let go* of the negative feelings, each time you exhale." (Pause one full minute)

Once you've regrouped, let's go back and have a look at what you were actually *feeling* during that exercise. I expect that you would have felt at least one of these — anger, annoyance, fear or confusion. Don't be concerned - you will know deep down exactly what it is that you felt, and the important thing to recognize is that what you felt was actually *negative energy*.

Think about what messages your heart received while you were remembering? What did your heart communicate to your mind? Did that memory cause the energy to feel nice, nurturing, healing? I would think that rather than feeling good, the energy felt wrong, bad, damaging and hurtful.

So the next question is how do we heal from negative feelings and learn from past experiences?

Well, you have already begun your journey to healing, even if it is not clear to you just how.

By simply going back over old memories (either by choice or when something triggers a memory recall), you *can* eventually reach a point where the pain associated with the memory is gone, where all that is left is the memory and the wisdom you gained from the lesson(s) learned are there for you to apply in the future.

This stage is the most important to get to in your journey to serenity. To be free of chronic emotional and physical pain associated with the memories of old events is the key to achieving inner harmony. When you feel inner harmony (and peace) so too will your relationships with others improve. It is a bit like 'paying it forward', but applied in a relationship context. Emotional intelligence and maturity will become your foundation stones for all relationships, and you will undoubtedly see huge improvements from that point on, in every context of your life.

Just imagine if all the angry people in this world were free of their emotional pain? What a blissfully happy world we would live in. There would be no more need for wars, for deceit, for retributions. Everyone would treat each other with kindness, compassion and courtesy, always. I would love that kind of world, wouldn't you?

[In Chapter 9 I explain more about why and how to let go of baggage (inner pain). You will find that Chapter very useful.]

Now let's look at *positive energy*. (Remember, either read this slowly and understand the steps, or have someone read it to you so you can focus on the doing.)

How do we recognize that inside ourselves?

(Positive energy – Exercise Two) "Take a minute to make yourself comfortable again. (Pause) Relax in an easy chair or lie flat on the floor, arms and legs uncrossed. Having your limbs open and free will help facilitate free energy flow through the meridians in your body.

Make sure your head is supported comfortably and your eyes are closed. (Pause) Relax your face. (Pause) Make sure the muscles in your face are really floppy.

Take some time now to find a memory of something truly pleasant, something that made you feel fantastic inside, full of life, happy and comfortable. (Pause) Spend several minutes remembering all the wonderful things. (Pause)

Remember the smells (Pause); remember the colors (Pause); remember the sounds (Long Pause).

Bathe in the beauty of those memories, allow the feelings to wander freely throughout your body, coursing where they need to go. Feel the energies stimulating and healing you (Pause). Listen to the sounds coming and going (Pause). Breathe deeply so that you can truly *taste* the smells (Pause).

Let the colors intensify and fade as they need to (Pause). Let your mind do what it needs to do to remember all those beautiful things.

Now focus on your heart. How does it feel? . . . . Warm . . . . Soft . . . . Blood flowing freely? . . . . (Long Pause) Gentle, easy, calm, regular beats? (Pause) Take some time to enjoy what your heart deserves to receive. (Pause at least one minute)

When you are ready, and only when you are ready, let your mind come back to the here and now (Pause). Focus on your toes . . . . make them wiggle (Pause). Now your knees . . . . give them a shake, up and down. Now focus on your hips and stomach . . . . What did you have to eat last? (Pause) Wiggle your fingers (Pause). Rock your neck gently and slowly from side to side . . . . breathe in and out deeply, open your eyes (Pause). Move your arms and shoulders a little. Breathe in and exhale strongly 2-3 times (Long Pause).

And when you are ready, sit up and feel yourself really back in the now."

How did that feel? Pretty fabulous?

Never forget, you are capable of delivering *so* much good, *positive energy* to yourself it's hard to imagine life without it, isn't it?

Imagine how good someone *else* will feel to receive a gift of your good, positive energy? Giving to another is not about channelling energy as a trained Reiki practitioner would do; that is different, in the universal energy sense. Channelling or giving another person some of your good, positive energy is simply about *being* in the moment with them; being tolerant, loving, kind, considerate, compassionate, understanding and empathetic; really listening to them, listening to what's in their heart. It's often times easier to be that way with ourselves as we have a natural self-protective instinct. By choice we humans would rather nurture than destroy our own being.

But giving and *being present* with another is a priceless gift that others will always remember you for. They will remember how you made them feel.

Actively listening is something some of you do all the time, often times with yourself! It's a bit like biofeedback, or self-love, isn't it? What we need to activate though, to make our world more harmonious and caring, is the giving of this positive focus to others around us. Giving to another person can be very easy, especially when we are not hurting inside ourselves. Giving to another person can also be very challenging. It takes every ounce of selflessness to still give to another human being when we are hurting about something that has happened to us or something that we have done that perhaps we should have done differently and now we feel guilty. But, when the challenge is overcome, either be it by waiting for the right time to give, or simply waiting for that person to come to us when they are ready to receive, it helps us to feel fulfilled and sound, and complete in every way.

It's pretty hard to imagine life without someone to give to, someone to share and enjoy life with. Many people live lives that are barren and dry of human interaction and that may be as a consequence of their choices in life (actions or words), or simply that they have little or no control over their circumstances. Someone else may have disempowered them. People caring for others, confined to prisons, institutions of care and hospitals, do not have full control of what happens to them and their opportunity to interact with others. Fortunately these folks are, fortunately, in the minority and for some their experience is only for a short time. But for others, disempowerment may have become chronic and crippling.

If you have an internally-imposed restriction, including where you have given someone else the control and power over decisions that impact directly on you, then it is you who can benefit most from a complete rethink of what it is that you need, deserve and want out of life (for yourself and others with whom you have a mutual responsibility or interdependency).

I talked earlier about how we humans deliver energy to the universe even while we sleep. Let's explore that more.

It is difficult, I know, to imagine creating positive energy inside while you sleep, but it is possible. What it requires is a conscious decision and steadfast focus on the outcome desired – a restful, happy night's sleep. If you are feeling tormented or anxious about something, mulling things over in your head, it is unlikely that your sleep will be restful. The key is in getting yourself to a level of understanding and calm *first*, and then staying with it, allowing the goodness and positive energy to permeate your body and conscious mind completely and fully, *prior* to sleep. Don't expect you will get there miraculously *while you're* sleeping; preparing yourself for a sound sleep is the key. Though, if you can facilitate self-hypnosis[5] that will certainly speed up the process.

For the vast majority of you, an exercise similar to the positive memory recall you did earlier is usually sufficient to establish a level of inner calm prior to going to sleep. If it doesn't give you enough of a sense of calm and there are still negative memories or thoughts in your head, you may prefer to use other methods, such as active reflection of the negative memories (such as we did earlier), receiving a massage, meditation, gentle exercise, singing, chanting, or even reading. Whatever nurtures and calms your soul at the deepest level (and you *will* know deep in your heart what that is) *is* the best choice. In Chapters 4 and 5 that follow you will learn more about how to find solutions within yourself. Always trust your self-protective and self-nurturing mechanisms to help your through this change journey.

Regardless of what time of day or night, the energy we are delivering not only impacts in the here and now, it has a strategic impact on events and people into the future. In every context the energy that we 'put out' becomes part of the broader energy pool – a bit like ripples on a pond reaching further and wider as they travel.

For example, you attend a meeting in a happy frame of mind but during the meeting someone criticizes something you've done. They have accused you of something that is not true, is not founded in fact and this discredits you in front of all those present. What do you do?

Do you argue with the person, loudly, abusively and allow the pain of their accusations to overrule logic (option one)? Or, do you listen to all they have to say, then calmly and quietly state the true facts drawing examples to reinforce your position, look them in the eye and hold firm in your resolve to see justice and truth emerge (option two)?

Option two is a far more effective, positive and lasting use of personal power than option one. The option one outburst, whilst

---

[5] Self-Hypnosis is a practice best done after much careful tuition and guidance

offering instant relief of inner pain, doesn't allow you to rationalize the situation and remedy the error.

What would be the longer term result if option one was chosen? Negative energy would fill the room, others present would actively switch off their capacity to hear all that's being said, the errors would not be corrected and the parties involved in the exchange of words would undoubtedly remain at odds with one another for a time. People would leave the meeting with mixed messages and form opinions that weren't founded in all the facts. They would make dangerous assumptions.

Option two however offers a more constructive and diffusing use of personal power, to the benefit of all present. What it relies on though is the personal power of the one being accused remaining strong under pressure, not giving in to another's negative use of personal power, holding true to what's right and just. The energy emitted as a counter measure is therefore a positive energy, one which will leave the others present at the meeting in a much more pleasant state of mind and being. Spectators to the exchange are more likely to actively listen to a person who remains calm, positive and firm. They will leave the meeting with a different impression about what just occurred and will form opinions based on all they had heard, not just the energy they felt.

THE ENERGY YOU PUT OUT INTO THE UNIVERSE HAS BOTH AN IMMEDIATE AND A STRATEGIC IMPACT

Another example: you witness the unrelenting verbal and/or physical abuse of a child by an adult. What do you do in that circumstance? Do you stand by and watch it happen, go home and talk about how bad it was and then wait for the next time you see the child become a victim of negative and destructive personal power (option one)? Or, do you remain calm and strong and, if a risk assessment reveals minimal risk to your own safety, confront the abuser and challenge their actions; and/or, where possible, report the abuser to the relevant authorities (option two)?

Option one is easy — you are being an observer in life, not getting involved, not protecting those who are unable to protect themselves. Option two, after careful risk assessment, is using your personal power in a very positive way; showing the abuser that you have the victim's interests at heart; that the victim has your support and you will not stand by and watch violence occur without helping to prevent it from happening again.

Before you can utilize your personal power in the most positive and constructive of ways, you must understand yourself at a deeper level — identify and understand your true motivations, needs and wants. Personal power is only of benefit to you and the human race if you use it willingly, wisely and with good intent.

Hold that thought, and we will explore the positive and negative uses of personal power in greater depth in Part 2.

CHAPTER 3

What is Positional Power?

Power is also described in the Encarta Dictionary as "control and influence over other people and their actions".

Positional power is made available through the formal, structural authority that a position, office or role brings. It's therefore not true to say that the higher up the position is depicted in a hierarchy, the more powerful that position is. Lower ranked positions can often wield greater power and influence over people and events by the very nature of the outcomes expected *of the position*.

It is true to say, though, that the most senior appointed person in a structure usually has right of veto over decisions, and thus is deemed to have the greatest positional power, when called upon by necessity. You will have heard the President of the United States of America (USA) say "I'll veto it". Such a position in world politics holds enormous (positional) power under certain circumstances.

Any head of Government is in place for a purpose - to make change. Some of you will advocate that the leader of the nation may only be there for selfish reasons, and you'd be quite accurate in your estimation of their minimal integrity. But, in countries where democracy rules, where the majority vote 'for the good of the people' is the foundation for rules and policies, the leaders are *more likely* to have others, not just themselves, in mind when making major decisions that affect the livelihood of the country, its people and ultimately the world's people.

When it comes to decisions that have strategic impact on a whole country, and perhaps the world, the most powerful person who, by rights, should have been elected into power on the basis of merit and with the confidence of the people, may stop something from happening if, in their judgment, it may have an adverse outcome. Some examples of this power of veto include:

- deployment of troops into hostile territories or on peace-keeping missions; or the withdrawal of same;
- creation or cessation of government services;
- provision of monetary aid to nations in need, or withdrawal of same;
- economic/trade sanctions;
- creating, and passing through for Government approval, new laws or their attendant regulations;
- the closure of major facilities or institutions; and/or
- the re-direction of government funds from one priority improvement area to another e.g. health system monies redirected to education; road maintenance monies redirected to research and development.

What may be clearly visible to some of you is that *strategic impact* is not even in the minds of many of our most powerful decision makers. Most of these decision-makers don't think beyond their current term of office and this is, unfortunately, quite selfish on their part. The importance of decisions that Government officials, and those who advise them, make should *never* be underestimated. Any decisions made by them will make or break a country's future and will have either a positive or negative global impact. Many of you will think "Sure Nola, we know that already", but have you *really* given it much of your mental energy, identifying ways you can make a personal difference so that the errors are not repeated through generations of politicians and government officials?

For me personally, I don't engage in game-playing of any kind and in any context. When necessary I question decisions made by anyone and everyone in positions of power (i.e. I use my personal power as the challenging tool), when I know or even sense that their decisions are based on:

- assumption(s), not fact;
- selfish motives (fear, control, bias, prejudice);
- greed;
- destructive intent;
- an injustice having been done to someone else; or
- their having discredited someone wrongfully.

Withholding your personal power when you know that those with positional power are doing wrong, is actually a grave misuse of your abilities and strength. Power mongers need to be challenged. People who do you wrong as a result of their position need to be challenged. Any leader worth his/her salt will stand up to a challenge and universal justice will prevail.

This is especially true when someone has been directed to perform a deed which is karmically wrong, but has no recourse in law to refuse the direction. Military folks are in this situation every day. They are required to follow direction or be charged under their respective military law for refusing to follow an order.

How we can get around this situation with a WIN/WIN outcome for all concerned, and improve karmic outcomes, will be discussed later in the book.

It is very clear when we observe those in positions of high authority, those *seen* as or expected to be leaders, that there are many who lack insight into their personal power (and therefore demonstrate little, if any, of the endearing qualities associated). These people need a position to give them power over others for they appear powerless without it. Think about Adolf Hitler and Napoleon. Their intent was pretty clear, but it was not an intent that meant positive strategic outcomes for our world. In Hitler's case, did he want to know about the harm he and his followers would do to generations and cultures beyond that of his own? It's most unlikely that he cared at all what negative impact he would have. It was all about him.

Power, cruelty and control were his true motives and, as the future unfolded after him, humans have come to understand the true meaning of the term megalomaniac and experience the fallout from so many other types of power mongers, so short-sighted and lacking in leadership that they do far more harm than good.

Think of the neo-Nazi movement – a movement that despises homosexuality and is racist beyond comprehension. What the neo-Nazis speak of is destruction. The only logical conclusion I can draw from their behavior is that they fear homosexuals, people of color and different cultures. Is their fear based on any real assessment of the risks they face? Whether homosexuality is your cup of tea or not, is irrelevant. I am heterosexual but have known several gay men in my time who proved themselves to be great friends.

Do the Neo-Nazis actually loathe homosexuals because they themselves have (closeted) homosexual tendencies, and choose to hide behind destruction and power talk instead of being authentic? Whatever the reason, the negative energy these kinds of hate groups emit, each time they seek to destroy and disempower, only serves to add to their pain and perpetuate the evilness of their actions.

Hitler was destructive. His followers were destructive. They all lacked insight and sufficient intelligence; were spineless, emotionally weak and lacking in real personal power.

Power mongers will always need a position of importance to feel powerful because they lack insight into and strength in harnessing and using their personal power, i.e. *they need positional power to make them feel powerful.* Power mongers lack the ability to motivate themselves and so having power over others (through their position) keeps them artificially motivated.

I know some of you know you have positional and personal power and some of you don't know enough about either, to know how properly to use them. You're not alone!

People who knowingly possess very high levels of personal power and use it to affect positive change in a variety of ways, without the support or weight of positional power for reinforcement, are worth every ounce of praise and support we can give them. The most notable examples of these kinds of folk are:
- the scientists who labor in their laboratories making discoveries of universal importance and benefit;
- writers, without being motivated by monetary reward, share their wisdom for the benefit of all;
- buskers who share their talents with the masses in the street;
- mentors who share their wisdom and experience to assist others to grow, achieve and mature;
- charity workers who are paid nothing or very little to work long hours, often under arduous conditions, and they do so out of love;
- entertainers who visit the ill and infirmed, or to raise funds for both global and local community betterment;
- self-motivated staff at the coalface in organizations, who work each day to produce outputs and outcomes for the common good, go home each day feeling fulfilled and happy; and

- volunteers who give freely of their time to help others and the community.

Those who possess great *personal power combined with positional power*, can thus bring about major, positive and lasting change in their spheres of influence. Take a moment to think of Martin Luther King, Mahatma Gandhi, Princess Diana and Nelson Mandela. They could have kept their views quiet and not acted for positive change, but instead they walked tall and strong to teach others how to think, reason, reflect and do it right.

Positions of authority and power bring high levels of responsibility and accountability and thus it's most appropriate that honesty, integrity, transparency and humility underpin your actions and words at *all* times. There is a societal expectation that you will 'tell the truth, the whole truth and nothing but the truth'. People are listening to you and will believe what you say. If you betray their trust, you will either have lost it forever or need to work very hard to win that trust back.

For you to stand in the face of others and 'expect' respect just because you hold a position of higher hierarchical authority, high public office, have more financial wealth, have just won a promotion, or have just married someone important, high profile or powerful, is a grave and naïve misuse of your personal power. No-one has the right to 'demand' respect from others just because of their position.

However, there are positions that automatically own a level of respect, regardless of the people who occupy them - these include royalty, the diplomatic corps and other dignitaries. The fine line here is the demanding or expecting of respect, which is a (negatively) forceful way of seeking the outcome, as distinct from simply 'being' the person in the position and letting the position deliver the respect that is customary.

Never treat others as lesser beings, *never* assume and *never* adopt the attitude "Do as I do, but not as I say". These are particularly fatal mistakes to make when holding a position of power.

We've all seen the examples of people walking around high as a kite 'on a power trip'. What message do they directly and indirectly send to you? That they think they are important now; that they are better than you in some way?

In the first place, they are never *better* than you. In the second place, why did it take a *position* of power and authority to make them feel powerful? Quite simply, they had not discovered their *personal power* first and therefore weren't 'powerful' without the position to back them up.

What is also important for you to realize about positional power is that whilst the position itself may be powerful, it is no more *important* than any other position. No one human being is more *important* than another — we are all equal as members of the human race.

Likewise, time is priceless and therefore no one person's time is more valuable than another's.

TIME IS PRICELESS

How many times have you called a meeting and people arrive late? They are showing you the greatest disrespect by not valuing your time as highly as they obviously value their own. Likewise you are showing the same disrespect if you're late and keep others waiting. There's no excuse for being late just for late's sake. It's not hip, it's not cool and it will win you zero goodwill in business or personal circles. Give an apology, postpone the meeting, call to say you are on your way and forewarn that you may be a little late — show some common courtesy. Courtesy costs nothing, except a tiny amount of your time. Considering time is priceless, what have you lost?

In most business environments office space is at a premium. Meeting and conference rooms are in demand and bookings are essential to secure a facility for your specific needs. What if your meeting runs over time and impinges on another booking? What would you say to the people waiting? Would you apologize for taking their time and space? To not apologize would be just as disrespectful as the examples of lateness given earlier.

What about being invited somewhere for dinner or away for the weekend and then not showing up? Would it be appropriate to ring your hosts and apologize, giving a valid and truthful reason for not being able to join them? Of course it would. To simply not show up, when you had the power to communicate your intentions, is a blatant display of disrespect for the feelings and efforts of others.

Have you ever said to someone "I'll call you back" or left a voice mail message on your phone that says "Please leave a message and I'll call you back", and then never called them? In families, business and also in social settings we see this disrespect being shown *all* the time. Granted, there are times when you may receive a call from someone whom you have asked never to contact you again and they forget that their call is unwelcome. Of course, that's an exception to the rule and you wouldn't be expected to call them back. But in every other case, if you do not intend to return all calls then don't say that you will.

It is as simple as this: do what you say you will do or don't say it in the first place.

CHAPTER 4

Self-Exploration – Recognizing Where You Are At

From conception you have heard and felt from the universe around you. From that seemingly silent place where you grew to become a functioning human being – able to breath, to communicate out loud, to love, to give – you have taken a most remarkable journey already. Are you pleased with who you are and what you have become?

For many, the answer will be "yes". But for others, the answer will be a resounding "no".

For many people the notion of looking 'within' implies that there is something not working quite right, or that something needs fixing. Well, you will discover below that this is not necessarily true. What I am talking about is accepting yourself fully and completely the way you are right now and then identifying what you would like to change to make yourself feel and be even better than you are right now.

Unless injury, disease or advanced old age causes otherwise, every day of your life you will wake up. In the very simplest of senses, how you feel when you wake is a reflection of your inner self – your feelings, motivations, sense of security and wellbeing, and your physical and mental health.

What motivates you to get out of bed, to feed yourself, get clean and dressed then embark on the day's chosen activities, is something no other person can own, produce or duplicate for you. It is yours. Likewise, how you feel each day is yours to *choose*. How you treat other people, how you treat animals and the environment, is all a matter of *choice*.

HOW YOU ARE AND WHAT YOU DO IS ALL A MATTER OF CHOICE

I have known many people in my life who have been and continue to be cruel to animals (usually pets). The reason they take their pain out on animals is no different to why they usually take their pain out on humans too. The only real difference is that animals aren't able to sue, they aren't able to speak out about the injustice, they're not able to alter their circumstances with quite the same control that a person can. Yes they can bite and hurt back — why wouldn't they? (..considering you have been their teacher and shown them how to treat others). We read about cruelty to animals all the time but what is really done about it?

In a domestic sense, abusing a pet animal is no different to abusing your human family members. After all, pets are usually a member of the family. The most unfortunate part is when you know you are treating them badly but you don't know how to change your behavior, or you're not learning relationship lessons quickly enough. Many wives will treat their husbands with denial of intimacy, rejection, rough talk, emotional manipulation, and physical or mental cruelty, JUST as easily as men do to women. The question you must ask yourself, if you are one of these abusers, is "Why do I choose to do this?" Cruelty and nastiness are choices that people can easily avoid. Your behavior is always a choice.

Many would advocate that women are subjected to more cruelty than men. I don't agree with this generality and explain why in my second book (short title: From PMS to PMA). In the context of power and control imbalances, which remain rife in our world no matter which country you live in, I remain somewhat disappointed by events such as International Women's Day.

Yes, there is such a thing as International Men's Day however it's not *recognized* in the same way or given as much emphasis. My fundamental issue with focusing on gender, rather than talent, lies in my question "why should women be given more recognition than men?" A day that recognizes one gender above another, simply tags women/men as special because of their *gender*, when the truth is that women are no more 'special' than men and vice versa. Did we have a 'day' that celebrated mankind's walk from the humiliations of serfdom and slavery and then hold onto it, celebrating it through the centuries? No. We just saw that turning point as part of humanity's bigger evolutionary journey — something had to change for the better, for mankind to progress to what it has become now.

Would it not be more appropriate for us to simply acknowledge differences and achievements in a much less divisive way? When we keep labelling universal change based on differences and allocate a specific day to remember over and over again, we never let go of the past. How can we forge strongly ahead to the future if we have to keep reminding ourselves publicly how far we have come? That's looking backwards for motivation, when in fact motivation is best maintained by looking forward. We are not able to change the past, just learn from it and move on.

What people should do is accept that a degree of progress has been made, be happy with the changes and then, leave it at that. In the case of International Women's Day, what good, other than the forced public acknowledgment of women's achievements, comes of celebrating a day *just for women*? We have progressed to the 21st Century! We no longer need the feminist movement of the 1960's and 70's to make a point about women's rights and the importance of equality for them. Women's rights are no greater in value than those of children and men! Women and men are making choices all over the world, right now, every minute. Women are Chief Executives, Prime Ministers, Queens, having dozens of babies in one lifetime, surviving crippling illnesses and injuries, quietly and publicly achieving, in every walk of life. Women have broken through glass ceilings that men have held over their heads and it's happening all over the world.

What I ask you to think about for a while is why do we have to have "advocates" for women when there are no such "advocates" for men? Most times, and simply due to historical habits and the fears of men in power, women in positions of power usually *do* have to work harder, longer and with less reward. Only a woman would know the real barriers that women face when building a business or running an organization. BUT, so too men face barriers in certain professions and roles where women have traditionally been more 'present and active'. Men have fought for years to be given the same carer rights as women, the same parental leave entitlements, and the same acknowledgment of their domestic and parenting skills.

Some women are denied opportunities, t i m e a n d t i m e a g a i n , but equally so (and in some cases more so) are men. I can guarantee, the most positively powerful women on earth are not feminists. Feminists are absolutely no different in their intentions as chauvinists; and we all know how women feel about chauvinistic men! Genuinely 'powerful' women do not wish to 'rule the world' and push their sex's cause before that of men. They are powerful in their femininity and work hard to be recognized, promoted and rewarded based on their true merit and ability, not just because of their gender. They have nothing to prove to anyone because they have learned how to use their *personal power* wisely and positively. The negative energy that a feminist puts out into the world is destructive, no differently than a chauvinist's energy!

Never forget, *when you push too hard to gain power, you actually lose it.*

WHEN YOU PUSH TOO HARD TO GAIN POWER, YOU ACTUALLY LOSE IT

The day we humans truly accept that each person is unique and special and that no one gender is more entitled or should receive more recognition than the other is the day we will have fully matured. The day we have an anti-violence ribbon that is colored *purple*, the good universal energy color, (not white) is the day we will have achieved recognition of the silent majority.

I am a woman and through my life I've witnessed so much cruelty by women towards women, it makes me sick. It is my long held belief that the people treated most cruelly throughout time have been men - men have been sent to war, pushed to succeed, pushed to support families, and constantly pushed by societies to be the best. Men subject each other to violence and outbursts (purely because they have not learned to heal themselves and channel their power in a positive way.)

To make matters worse, the vast majority of men have been subjected to the cruelty of women, via the excuses of Pre-menstrual Syndrome or hormonal imbalance, all their lives. From women in their closest circles (mothers, sisters, wives, daughters) to women in their workplaces and social circles, men have endured far more than they would ever admit to and it is no wonder we have such a backlash happening when men and women feel disempowered by the other gender.

In my book *From Pre-Menstrual Syndrome to Positive Mental Attitude*, women and men are both taught more about how to heal themselves, improve their relationships and create lasting change for the betterment of humankind. And, in Part 3 (here) I hope to open your eyes to how men can heal themselves and achieve a lasting and positive impact on the world.

But for now, let me reflect on a story that dates back to c. 2001: I worked with two male colleagues, both around 50-55 years of age at the time. At different times and in different contexts they expressed both anger and surprise at my happiness with life, my positivity, and my love for people in general. On arriving at work one morning I recall one saying "No-one has a right to look that radiant". I thought to myself "Why not?"

On the other occasion I was asked why I was happy. My reply was simply "I just am". The return look of cynicism and doubt said it all. A few years later I revisited some old friendships from the 60's and 70's and found many of the women and men from then to be similarly programmed — full of criticism for others and about life in general, bullying and controlling in their behavior and dialogue, cynical and inconsistent about the success and motivations of others and themselves, and motivated first and foremost by personal gain. Displaying many of the characteristics of losers in life, not winners.

For a while I pondered why these people I'd once seen as happy and motivated held such negative responses to life and why they couldn't accept my choices to be happy, joyful and not 'stressed'. After a lot of reflection I concluded that they had long ago made their choices, they worked hard to control and manipulate others by their outlook, behavior and attitudes, and in summary were not people I wanted in my life on an ongoing basis.

Whether what you are experiencing in your life right at this second is good or bad, time always reveals the truth. Truth will emerge as a karmic lesson, in this lifetime or the next, to correct your wrongdoing or to awaken you to a reality you have not yet faced, but need to.

A work colleague I thought I knew back then, over time grew to reveal himself to be unbelievably self-centered and controlling beyond all reasonableness. Misogynistic in his tone, with a personality disorder clearly evident. His whole working life had been in the military, his home, and he dared not stray from the comfort zone of command and control. Unfortunately he could not separate the work part of life from non-work. His restrictive behaviors and attitudes had progressed him to only a certain point in his career (middle management), and he was frustrated not to be given opportunities or be listened to anymore (was he ever listened to?). In his private life he actively bossed people around, was easily angered, short-tempered and held lots of grudges, pushed hard for others to do things that he thought was right for them (even if they didn't), lied constantly and then laughed the lies off as just "a joke".

What intelligent person would lie and then say "Oops, I was only kidding!"? Telling the truth first and always is, by far, the best, long term solution. Tact, diplomacy, compassion and care must *always* underpin the truth. Without these positive karmic undercurrents truth becomes totally and completely destructive.

So many times I have heard people describe themselves or be described as cynics, eccentric, cursed, possessed, the devil incarnate or worst of all, evil. Some behavior may be evil but I would contend that a person *learns* to be evil through watching others and making bad choices; they are not born that way.

Why do people hold such a low opinion of themselves or not allow others to really see and experience their goodness? Fundamentally, it's because people believe that being negative, evil, scary (to others) and a "devil's advocate" gives them power. But, how wrong they are.

When you hear the term "goody two shoes" - what do you think? Of someone with squeaky clean integrity? Why is it that we routinely condemn and criticize goodness, purity and wholesomeness and yet sanctify those with negative traits and attitudes? In Australia, for as long as I've been alive, the term "tall poppy syndrome" is used to describe the toxic outcome of a high achiever being ripped down by those of lesser integrity or ability. Australians are very good at knocking others who do better, yet on the other hand Australians usually stand by their friends, their mates, at a time of crisis. So why the inconsistency? In the USA, efforts and achievements are usually celebrated. Why do Australians feel the need to belittle high achievers?

Deep inside yourself, whether you consciously recognize it or not, are the answers to why you do or don't do certain things, why you feel a certain way one time and not another. For example, that last job you didn't apply for, that last charity you didn't donate to, that last person you didn't engage in conversation with, that last risk you didn't take, that last smile you didn't give — why didn't you?

The reasons why are always within you, and it is important for you to understand and accept that *your decisions each day are the right decisions for you, at that time.* Hopefully you took all factors into consideration before you made your decision, assessed all the risks, and understood fully your motivations behind the decision. If not then you will learn the value of being this thorough, for if something backfires when you least expect it, the lesson can be doubly harsh. When you don't assess the likely impact of a decision made (a risk taken) and it has catastrophic results, it's sometimes impossible to recover from the situation and make right the wrong.

For example, you withhold information from someone or deliberately mislead them to believing one thing when the opposite is true. Firstly, this sets up foundation principles of dishonesty and manipulation between you both. Would that be good for a long term positive outcome? Of course not. Secondly, you are showing disrespect and a lack of trust in the other person when you don't share the truth and have your motives transparent and clear for the world to see.

A former friend told me once he only told little white lies. I said to him that to lie means that he has no idea what is really the truth in his mind and therefore I couldn't count on *anything* he said as believable. I then asked him how he felt after he lied and he said he always confesses, straight away. My question to you is, what's the point of lying in the first place? What purpose does it serve other than to waste time, cause confusion, perpetuate mind games and put negative energy into the universe? His continual lies were the foundation for my choice not to have him as a friend anymore. I've never regretted that decision (and to this day, do not recall his name). I have, however, remembered the lesson.

We hear people say "The truth hurts, so it's best to tell a lie" or "You always hurt the one you love the most. Lies are OK". If you look closely at the people who say these things you will undoubtedly see selfishness, cruelty, and/or disrespect as likely causal factors. Perhaps they have been lied to and think it's OK to do the same. Perhaps they think little of the person they lie to or are cruel to, and therefore boldly go ahead and put out negative energy without caring about the consequences to themselves or others. Whatever the root cause for their attitude and behavior, only a negative outcome will come. Without truth there can be no trust.

WITHOUT TRUTH THERE CAN BE NO TRUST

There are also those who will lie to deliberately mislead someone who is getting a little too close to the truth. When this happens you'll undoubtedly see the liar shy away from the person who challenges them, because after all a lie is a conscious attempt to deceive someone by deliberately saying something untrue.

Many people will tell you they lie very well, that they are the best liars in the world. Many men freely admit to lying and some women lie equally as well, when it suits them, so it is not a gender-based character flaw. The worst part is that lying is *universally accepted* as the norm in business, in families, and in social relationships. People accept that the world is largely an immoral place and don't seem to care to do anything to change that at an individual level. It is always "someone else's problem, not mine" they say.

So what is the result when your lies and deceit are discovered? Apart from a damaged (and possibly irrecoverable) relationship with the other person, your integrity and trustworthiness may always live under a questioning cloud of suspicion. Is that how you want others to see you? What is it that you feared the most by telling the truth and being open? Rejection? Exposure? Being seen as weak?

Remember, always . . . . when you lie or do not make right the wrong, negative karma will come back. It may not be in this lifetime, but it will come back and your soul will pay a dear price for your errors.

WHEN YOU LIE OR DO NOT MAKE RIGHT A WRONG, NEGATIVE KARMA WILL COME BACK

When I was 23 years old I was offered what to most young people in the computer industry would have been almost the 'perfect' job — Marketing Manager South East Asia, based in California USA, working for a multi-national computer company that I'd been professionally associated with for quite a few years. I verbally accepted the position but when it came to signing the letter of offer two weeks later I withdrew my acceptance.

It took many years before I really understood the key reason why I turned the job down. At the time I knew that choosing to work in California meant I had to give up working in New York City, the original location I'd been offered. In the early 1980's being Aussie in the USA was different, but in business different wasn't always an advantage there. I knew I would have to change in order to fit in and remain competitive in a demanding environment.

It wasn't until the early part of this century that I realized the underlying reason for my having turned that job down some 20 years earlier. It was fear. There were some personal concerns I had about a certain person in the management team - not knowing his true motivations. But above all I felt fear of being publicly recognized for what I had achieved in my short life.

In other words, I didn't feel that that level of recognition was deserved, even though it obviously was because that is exactly what the universe had delivered to me. I had been programmed (by others) to believe less of myself and despite having repeatedly proven my abilities (including achieving a senior leadership position at the age of 19) the speed of my second rise was astounding to me.

My choice to turn down the position in California was perfectly right at that time, (it was my only safe option) however had I had the level of self-awareness then that I do now, I could well have made different choices. And what the realization (years later) did was help me to identify and remove the barriers that I had previously placed in front of myself at times throughout my life. I learned to really value my contribution to life and others, and also learned to harness and more effectively and intuitively channel my personal power.

I learned a lot as a remedial therapist running a private clinic during the 90's. I counselled many clients with the specific goal of assisting them to recognize the emotional barriers to their physical ailments and rehabilitation. I helped them to understand that the body manifests what the mind visualizes - the concept of 'you are what you believe', and that the body (and mind) can also begin to heal once the conscious mind recognizes the root cause of barriers, pain and dysfunction. Whether healing from an injury or deciding a future path in life, the real barriers to your progress and the answers to facilitate change come from within you!

THE REAL BARRIERS TO OUR PROGRESS LIE WITHIN

The emotions and attitudes that sit beneath and alongside physical disease are very interesting. The stomach is often associated with decision making and, for many of you, when important decisions are being made or you feel 'stressed', you can experience physical symptoms like stomach upsets, heartburn, stomach ulcers and the like.

The elimination of emotional baggage (as we will explore in much more detail in Chapter 9) is often times linked to diarrhoea and, for the reverse where you are holding onto baggage, constipation. Toxic, negative thoughts can manifest as bad breath. Pushing too hard with your thinking can manifest itself as a migraine or headache. Resentment and blame ('the gall of them' type reaction) can manifest as liver or gall bladder-centric pain or pain around the temples and on the sides of the crown of the head.

If you have the chance, learn more about energy meridians, which are carefully mapped internally and externally in our bodies. What you will learn is that there are points along each meridian where energy can be skilfully stimulated (using massage, acupressure or acupuncture) to achieve balance and harmony in the body and the mind. Negative energy can be diffused. Positive energy can be heightened. When you learn your own touch-points you will then have the knowledge to give yourself a 'self-tune-up', and your body and mind will be the better for it.

It is very important for me to reinforce at this stage how critical it is for you not to self-diagnose and to seek medical treatment when necessary. There are medical tests specifically designed to diagnose illness and disease and, as pain is the last indicator that there is something wrong, it's vital that you consult with your chosen medical/health practitioner when pain persists. The body gives warning signs. For you to ignore them is foolish, potentially fatal and of grave disservice to the many people around you who wish to see you live a full, healthy and happy life.

When it comes to admitting something needs attention, you may hesitate as (particularly if you are a man) you may have been conditioned not to complain, told to "toughen up", told not to be a "cry baby". So many people hesitate to say how they really feel and it's such a shame.

There's a line in the movie Two Weeks' Notice where one male character says that all men are pawns when it comes to women; that all women do is make men talk about their feelings until the breath is sucked out of their body. That the man has to be in control . . . .

As much as I think that movie has some wonderful messages about doing good instead of evil, those particular lines are a load of rubbish. Yet how many people, of any age, will now believe that theory to be true of men and women just because it was in a movie and someone famous said it?

The makers of movies, authors of books, and headline hunting journalists have much to answer for. They should reflect more closely what huge strategic harm they are doing to the human race and our interrelationships, when they allow false beliefs and unfounded rubbish to perpetuate.

Every statement that you make has the potential to influence others. Therefore, think and listen twice, and speak once.

THINK AND LISTEN TWICE - SPEAK ONCE

It is always refreshing to hear a man talk about his feelings, without shame, guilt or fear, and then allow others to empathize with him. When a man is this honest he is opening himself up to the goodness and positive power of those around him. If someone asks you how you are and you are honest in your reply e.g. "tired, stressed and about had a gut full; but apart from that I feel great", then you can walk tall with a huge sense of comfort, relief and freedom. You have said it like it is. You are being truly authentic.

Lying is all about withholding your personal freedom. Whilst ever you stay stuck in lies, deceit and manipulation mode you will never be truly free.

How convenient and selfish is it that churches benefit from the sins of others? Why would religions wish to perpetuate human wrongdoing (lying etc.) and the need for confession of sins and spiritual cleansing, other than to ensure their ongoing existence? From the point of view that 'prevention is much better than cure', it would help our world immensely for people to simply stop lying! Truthfulness is not hard. It just takes courage and determination to uphold that value against *all* those who discredit you for being honest and who mock your inner strength and resolve.

We see books like "Why Men Lie and Women Cry . . . ." and "Men Are From Mars, Women Are From Venus" that perpetuate the belief that women and men are wired differently, have different emotional needs and that there is nothing that can be done to change this. The important thing to understand is that humans are *programmed* or conditioned differently, based on our genetic makeup and experiential learning. We may have different tendencies and preferences, but *we are not wired differently.* We are all human beings of the same species after all.

Our behaviors and attitudes will differ and, by choice, we allow ourselves to be influenced by what is transmitted or distributed to us via books, the media, schools, business entities and the Internet, f o r e x a m p l e ; but, fundamentally our essence as humans is the same. You have a physical and spiritual structure that is fundamentally the same as the next person. The only exceptions are for gender-specific functional structures or differences that emerge as a consequence of familial genetics, conception, foetal development, and/or life experience (and thus spiritual changes).

In Chapters 6 and 7 you will learn more about life and societal conditioning and how what we 'learn' leads us to believe nonsense, emotive things that are not founded in any scientific fact.

One of the hardest, and yet most rewarding, things you can do is to explore why you feel a certain way. At times you will wonder after making a decision, whether it was the right decision. Reflection is a reasonable and normal thing to do; rationalizing behaviour, action and inaction is all part of the learning experience. You make value judgments about things every day. Often times though, when you are unsure about a decision made, or an action taken or not taken, it is worthwhile to dig deep within yourself to understand your motivations and identify root causes for the barriers that you feel are there. Let's work through some scenarios to explain this process of self-exploration:

Scenario One: You have just arrived home and your spouse is upset with you. You're ignored, given the cold shoulder and genuinely feel hurt by the lack of interest and response. Why do you feel hurt? Let's say the questions and your answers flow something like this:

"Because I've had a bad day and need someone to talk to."
Why do you need someone to talk to?
"Because I don't like being alone."
Why don't you like being alone?
"Because I'm frightened on my own."
What are you frightened of?
"I don't know."
Are you sure?
"Well, actually I'm afraid that I won't be heard, that people won't listen."

Now that you have worked out why you feel that way, perhaps it's time you helped your spouse explore the reasons why they are upset.

Scenario Two: You have to deliver some bad news to someone and feel awful for being the messenger. You know they are very distressed as a result of the news.

Why are you feeling bad about delivering the message?
"Because I would rather someone else do it."
Why would someone else doing it make it any easier on the person receiving the news?
"It wouldn't, it would just get me off the hook."
Why do you want to be off the hook?
"Because I don't like delivering bad news, only good news."
Why is that?
"I don't know; maybe it's because when people have delivered bad news to me they seemed not to care how I felt."

It's pretty clear the past has dealt you some hard blows. Perhaps it's time for you to heal from the past and let go of the baggage.

Scenario Three: You have just been told you have a terminal illness and must inform your family of the news. You are very concerned about the impact the news will have.

Why are you concerned?
"Because no-one is able to change the outcome and they might abandon me."

Why do you think they'll abandon you?

"Because they know I won't be around much longer and I don't like the thought of them leaving me to fight this on my own, to fend for myself."

Why will you have to fend for yourself?

"Because that's how it's always been. When I get in a scrape, people don't help me."

All these scenarios point to root causes that are founded in memories of past events. Most people will say it is from the past that we learn. That is true; understanding usually comes from experience and wisdom comes after we apply the learnings from our mistakes. However, always remember that the past will never repeat itself. It is not possible to exactly duplicate the past as time has already moved things forward and changes have occurred. Nothing you do now can change what you did, said or thought a second ago. We are always stepping into the future, with every breath. And as we deliver actions and words to the now, we set in place a path to the future.

AS WE DELIVER ACTIONS AND WORDS IN THE NOW, WE SET A PATH TO THE FUTURE

Thought processes and decisions that take you outside your comfort zone are often difficult at first, aren't they? Feeling totally comfortable with who you are, what you have done or not done, what effect or impact you have on other people and letting go of the pain associated with the past are important steps in the journey to self-realization.

Self-realization comes when you trust in the decisions you make as being the right decisions at the time and that, as a result, you have grown as a person, as a member of your community and as a member of the human race.

CHAPTER 5

What Do I Need and Want?

At various stages of our lives we re-evaluate what is most important, what brings us joy and fulfilment, what is critical to our happiness and to our survival and growth.

Who and what is most important to you? Is it marrying that special someone, a bigger pay check, a promotion, the opportunity to share with others, a chance to do something good for humanity, being heard, a holiday, recognition for your efforts, a hug, or a smile? Take time now to list all those people and things that are vitally important to you now and into the future.

Take a moment to reflect on what you wish to see happen, what needs to change, what do you need for yourself or would love to see for others[6]? Structure the list to reflect short, medium and long term (life-long) goals. Group similar subjects together as topics if necessary. Make headings — personal, work, family, friends, financial, career etc. Whatever helps you to better understand your needs and wants.

Focus on your *needs* first, the foundation rocks that are critical to your happiness. The soul nurturing wants should come next. I do recommend you leave the superficial wants off th list, as they're not important in the big scheme of things.

---

[6] Be very careful to understand your motives here. Do you actually want to control an outcome for someone else? This is not your place!

Now that you've done that, prioritize the list. Start with the most critical or recent, working your way to the least critical or furthest in distance. Be specific and succinct about what you wish to see happen but do not limit any unforeseen opportunities. For example, if you have recently applied for several new jobs and any one of them would be a great choice, don't be specific about only one job from that list. Simply state "to win one of the new jobs I have applied for" is sufficient to start the universal ball rolling and generic enough that the one that is best for you, at this point in time, will be the one you choose when it is offered. If you specify a particular job by title, then if that's not offered to you, the others are less likely to be either. They won't have been included in your life plan, will they?

The most important thing to remember when writing your strategic life plan is to set the vision for the future — what are the 'now' changes that will make the future vision become reality? What is it that is closest to your heart's desire? What do you really want to make happen? Use visualization techniques to establish in your mind's eye exactly what you want, then document those needs and wants in the strategic life plan. Be brave. Ask for what you really want; what you believe you deserve as reward for all your effort; what resonates well for you.

MAKE A STRATEGIC 'LIFE' PLAN AND CELEBRATE SUCCESSES

A life plan could look like this:

Personal	Career/Work
1. Lose 12 pounds within one year and improve my fitness 2. Spend more leisure time with immediate family 3. Take time out to visit with friends 4. Learn to cook Mexican food 5. Take a holiday to Europe within five years 6. Pay off the house mortgage before retirement 7. Do charity work when I retire	1. Secure a job in Marketing within two years 2. Gain a promotion to Manager within three years 3. Start and grow my own business by 30 4. Join a professional association or industry body and remain actively involved

Make sure the list is realistic, achievable, doesn't ask for everything at once (i.e. sets goals to be achieved over time), and is morally and legally correct. Keep it simple, not complex.

Make sure you don't write things like "See so-and-so's business flourish" because that is actually attempting to control someone else's life. They may well wish to sell the business, not grow it. How do you know what's in their mind and what *their* plans are? You're not able to read their mind and are not them, so don't ever presume to know what is best for them. You are you. Only control your outcomes.

When you know you are in a partnership for life, work with your partner to write the strategic life plan. After all, it is by mutual agreement that shared dreams and goals are achieved.

Amend the list each day or so until you know it reflects your true desires and resonates well for you and, once complete, refer to the list as often as necessary to reinforce the goals and changes you have set in motion. As circumstances change or goals are achieved, revise the list, add new goals or re-prioritize if need be. Make this a living strategic plan for your life and above all else, celebrate all successes along the way.

Why should we celebrate successes? Because they are achievements, be they small or large, that deserve recognition in the here and now. Celebrating successes generates a positive, joyful foundation for the future. To allow an achievement to go by without acknowledging the goodness it brought, automatically devalues the outcome as something relatively insignificant.

Rewarding effort and celebrating successes is critical in both the business world and in your private life. The mere act of celebrating brings people together in a positive way, helping them to see happiness in life and a reward for their efforts. Only goodness will come of that.

CHAPTER 6

Internal Programming

At conception your essence was founded, your soul had a place to reside and grow. Your physical body and your mind began to develop at an astonishing rate.

Research is still underway regarding the emotional and spiritual journey undertaken by a foetus in utero. It is clear though that from conception to approximately age seven is the most critical time for human beings to learn moral standards, attitudes and establish a value system. A human being's experiences and what is recorded on their inner 'tape' — the unconscious or subconscious mind — right through life from conception will have a direct impact on their ability to function in society as a rational, loving and reasonable human being.

With few exceptions (such as a baby born of a drug-dependent or infected mother) the vast majority of people are born positively 'programmed'. A mother's experience of and during pregnancy is a very powerful foundation for the new born baby's state of mind and emotional wellness. Babies are generally born happy, loving, communicative and gentle. Babies are not born with prejudices, fears, biases, etc. They learn these.

Prejudices, fears, biases etc. are *programmed* into people, based on experiences and contact with other people. By the time many people die, they have eroded levels of happiness, lack gentleness, communicate less, are not as loving as earlier in their lives, and carry loads of emotional baggage. Why?

The answer is quite simple. They choose to be that way. They choose to hang on to their pain.

BABIES ARE NOT BORN WITH PREJUDICES, FEARS AND BIASES – THEY LEARN THEM

From conception, the messages you receive are processed by your conscious mind and then selectively stored in your subconscious. The subconscious mind is the filing system for experiences. It holds the memories, and for many people the associated pain, which the conscious mind has decided will need to be recalled, and used to validate or benchmark against, at a later time. It is the powerful inner 'tape' that maintains the broad record of your life, reinforces the negative or positive mindset that you *choose* to adopt, and thus forms the foundation for your conscious decision making.

Messages delivered by others on a daily basis will either be positive, negative or a combination of both. The way our subconscious is programmed, and our chosen mindset, will dictate the dialogue we engage in and our responses to communication by others.

For a few months in 2006 I worked near a man (mid 40's) who was negative, sexist, bored, sour-faced, cynical, lazy, self-pitying or unhappy – *everyday, by choice*. He found it impossible to rise above negativity and just 'be happy'. A few times you could see him struggling to act happy; a fleeting moment of light put out by his overpowering negative mindset! He found it almost impossible to smile. And when he was challenged for his attitude and negative, sexist comments he would become even worse. The more negative he saw the outside world and those around him, the harder it was for him to feel comfortable in the largely positive friendly environment. The positive was literally choking him to death.

He was suffocating.... because he was unable, and unwilling, to accept alternatives.

His colleagues said it was because his wife left him after they moved interstate, but isn't that just an excuse? What right did he have to subject people around him to his negative energy and emotional baggage? Negativity is toxic to positive people.

Likewise he felt confronted and suffocated because others' positivity was equally toxic to him. He was overwhelmed by internal negative and felt enormous pain from the memories he wouldn't *allow himself to heal from*.

Next time you listen to the news on television or the radio, hear the negative. How much positive is there to balance the negative out? Not much, is there?

Tony Blair, the most vocal of many global leaders, visited the Middle East war zone prior to his departure as Prime Minister of the United Kingdom. He condemned the press for publicizing only the negative aspects of what was occurring in countries being rebuilt; and not sharing the positive.

The media makes money off sensationalism, lies, exaggerations and humiliations. What good does this serve for the human race into the long term? Negative is *programming* the consumer and they will then look for more negative information.

Accepting negative communication (through any medium) and building negative dialogue within, appears to be the 'norm' for many people. Certainly most psychologists will advocate that negative motivation is more powerful than positive. But, isn't that just another way of perpetuating what really needs to change? It takes much more effort to change from doing things the wrong (negative) way, to doing things right (and positively). When we make this choice to positivity, our efforts will bring humankind astoundingly positive results. The knock-on effect is almost instantaneous.

Negative begets negative. If you receive only negative that is what you are most likely to look for, and that is how you will communicate to your own subconscious and to other people. If the majority of messages you receive during your lifetime are negative, cruel and destructive messages, your mind will be *programmed* to see this as normal. Whereas, positive messages that people communicate will be perceived by you as *not* normal. Hence your sense of confusion and surprise when positive people communicate with you consistently that way every day.

As parents we have enormous power over our children — to help them to grow and learn, keep them safe from harm, influence their thinking and behavior, even direct them down a certain path to the future. It is how you use that power and the messages you convey that will influence your child's internal programming, their effectiveness as an adult, and their ability to relate constructively to others.

For example: a parent says to their 10 year old son "See you soon rat bag."

What subliminal message does that send?

The son will automatically view himself as naughty, needing punishment and not be in your favor.

So often parents use these 'cute' little phrases without realizing they are programming their children every step of the way, setting them up for insecurity and lowered self-esteem as they get older.

Telling your young son "Don't be a girl" when he is upset and crying makes for nothing but confusion in your son's head. Firstly, your son knows he's not a girl so why confuse his mind with something that will never be true. Secondly, crying doesn't make you a girl. All humans cry when they need to — it's normal. Thirdly, why would you seek to infer that a girl is not like a boy in their responses to things when, in fact, they are both human beings?

How many times do you hear a parent say "Don't be stupid" over and over again, year in year out? That very phrase labels the *person* as stupid, programming them to believe they are not clever, not able to reason very well and generally unintelligent. What would be better to say is "That was stupid", which correctly identifies the *behavior* as undesirable, ill-thought or wrong, not the person. The programming outcomes will be entirely different in these two instances. One will cause grave long term damage. The other will have long term positive impact if followed up with consistency and the parents leading by example.

The work associate I mentioned earlier would often say to himself "You're a twit!" What he was inadvertently doing was programming himself (using negative internal dialogue) to reinforce his feelings of inadequacy. But was he really inadequate? Or had someone else said those things to him long enough, and frequently enough, for him to actually believe they were true and he chose to keep reminding himself?

It would be safe to conclude that his feeling that way about himself is likely founded in other people's programming of him at a young age, and unless he were to journey under hypnosis and recall the memories, he is unlikely ever to *consciously recognize* that this damage was done very early in his life.

What about when a child says to their unhappy parent "You're crazy". How would a child know what is crazy and what is not? Where would a child get that from, unless from peers, other family or friends? The child is showing a significant disrespect to the parent and the parent *must* be consistent in their return messages that they are not crazy and will not tolerate such abuse. The power of a child to damage a parent is very clear. Parents usually strive to do everything right by their children and to be verbalized in such a manner is a negative use of the child's personal power. But the child must have learned it somewhere, so it is up to the strong parent to keep correcting the negative programming.

To tell someone who loves you deeply and wants the best for you, whether individually and together, that "It's all in your head" is one of the cruelest things you can say. You are countering their positive thought processes with your negative.

Perhaps you don't want to see or believe in the same things as them. That's fine. But say "That's not what I want", instead. Don't put the blame on them. Accept and act on your right to refuse and say the truth. That is what's best in the long run.

When Hitler started chanting his beliefs, over and over, louder and louder, what did people do? They listened, some in fear, and others, simply because they believed what he said was feasible, achievable and morally right. We all know what Hitler wanted and did was immoral, insane, inhumane and of grave strategic impact to humanity, but he still managed to program and indoctrinate people everywhere he went. He used whatever means available to force his message onto others. He used threat of reprisal action, intimidation, and every word he could summon from his toxic brain, to perpetuate evil thoughts and actions. Only a coward perpetuates evil and he has gone down in history as one of our worst, most toxic cowards.

Think about his power . . . . did he use his personal power for any good at all? . . . . Of course not.

So how do you know what mindset you are in?

Here are some simple examples of equivalent messages, differentiated by the mindset of the *communicator* (the person communicating to others):

Positive (Motivated) Mindset	Negative (Doubtful) Mindset
Challenge; temporary barrier or obstacle	Problem
Will/Am	Try
Let's watch this space	Don't hold your breath
Fantastic; Terrific; Great; Outstanding	Not too bad
When	If; maybe
Advocate or negotiate (for)	Argue (for)
Expect/Foresee that; or Allow/Provide for (whichever the context)	Assume (that)
I eagerly await the outcome	I'll believe it when I see it
I'll help you	I'll wait to see if you can put your money where your mouth is first

In everyday communication, is someone says "We need to argue our case . . . ." a simple adjustment to "We need to negotiate our case . . . ." changes the dialogue to positive and sets an entirely different scene for both the communicator and the *communicatee* (the person receiving the communication). There is no longer a perceived winner and loser; the adversarial and aggressive approach is removed. By using the right words and projecting a positive mindset, you will set a much better foundation for a positive **WIN/WIN** outcome.

In every aspect of life you are receiving direct and indirect (subliminal) messages. For all your life you have been watching, listening and learning — from everyone around you; from people in positions of influence and power; your wider family, friends, business associates, and children.

Our response(s) to what people communicate, no matter how they communicate, is dependent on our mindset. If you are in a negative mindset, you will receive the communication the opposite way to if you are in a positive mindset. You will likely hear a simple comment or observation as a major criticism — every time.

Positivity is infectious and powerful, but so is negativity. The ultimate choice of how to 'think and be' is yours and yours alone. Unwarranted criticism or punishment, ridicule, abuse, blame and admonishment, of yourself or others, is the total opposite of positivity.

For example: If you're in a negative mindset and a colleague says to you "Joseph has done a great job with that report!" you'll probably think "But I do a great job too. Why don't you see that I am just as good as Joseph?"

When in a positive mindset you'll likely think "Yes he did, and I am happy that Joseph is being given that recognition."

If you are in a negative mindset and your husband says to you "You look different today honey." You'll likely think "What's the matter with me? He doesn't like my hair; he doesn't like my shoes. Oh, I can never please him!"

When in a positive mindset you'll likely think "Yes, I do look good. Terrific, he is noticing me. I'll have to do this more often!!"

When in a negative mindset you are always looking for someone to find fault with what you are doing or saying; you'll tend to be cynical about and untrusting of others; and you could even dump on yourself, subconsciously, almost every minute of the day. You'll likely find it hard to smile, or be happy with life, or feel fulfilled and motivated.

When you get like this, take a minute to check out how many people are milling around you. Not many? After all, you are being perceived as a loser in life. But is that really fair?

A negative mindset is something we're all capable of slipping into from time to time, and life does deals us challenges that can have our heads and hearts spinning in confusion and pain. The key is whether you *choose* to stay in the negative mindset. It's never permanently programmed in, so you can step into the positive *any time you like*.

When in a positive mindset you'll likely be constantly validating yourself, giving yourself pats on the back, feeling happy with your accomplishments. You won't look for validation from others. You'll be winning in life all by yourself. And, as a result of winning for yourself, you can easily and without much effort, acknowledge when those around you are winning too.

POSITIVITY IS INFECTIOUS AND POWERFUL AND WHEN YOU ARE WINNING IN LIFE YOU CAN EASILY HELP OTHERS TO WIN

So what is winning all about?

Quite simply, it's an attitude. It's the mental and emotional posture you adopt in approaching each new day with an open heart and mind. You can be having the worst day, people can be constantly interrupting you, you can stub your toe on a chair, but you can still be winning!

Why?

Because it's all about how you *see* what is happening that counts. It's your attitude to life that makes or breaks.

To me, winning is about waking up alive every day with a smile on my face, knowing I'm loved and that I love others dearest to me. It doesn't matter that the day is sunshine or rain, cold or hot, weekend or workday. I rejoice at being alive, healthy and happy.

The simple truth to hold faith about, is that out of *every adversity, something of goodness will come*. Even the death of a loved one, the ending of a relationship or association, leaving a job, suffering illness or injury, will result in something positive in the future. What you must learn to do is look for and grow the positive outcome(s), not focus on the negative.

Constantly wallowing in self-pity is a self-destructive and selfish past time, which does nothing to change things for the better. Sure, you may like the sympathy that others give you, for a while, but aren't you just feeding negativity to yourself, reinforcing a negative mindset?

I'm sure that some of you will not yet fully recognize what your internal programming is, but you *will* in time. Sometimes a positive person will actually tell you that you're being negative. You'd best listen when that happens and learn from them quick smart. Assessing the reaction of others to things that you say is a pretty useful way to gauge if you've said something negative or in a destructive way. It is everyone's right to say negative things, when warranted, but it is *how* you say it that counts.

The other way to understand your mindset is to gauge if people you know to be very positive are still having contact with you. Perhaps you have fallen back into the wasteland of negativity and need a reality check.

Your reality check might come when they disappear out of your life.

The exercises of delving deep within to identify why you feel a certain way, recognizing root causes for the emotional barriers that you have built over time, will definitely help you gain a much greater insight into your internal programming and the power of your mindset. You will see how certain events, such as death or parting of a loved one, will cause your mindset to swing to the negative for a while. You must trust though that, over time, you will be able to lift yourself out of the negative mindset, back to the positive.

If you know you have a negative mindset and your programming has been largely negative all your life, and if you want to change to be positive again, then make a decision to change right now. Don't put it off to another day. The longer you allow negative to influence and control your life, the longer and harder the journey back to the positive.

I'd like to share a couple of examples from my own high school years so that you can see the application of mindset and how important self-belief is. . . .

In my first year of high school (in Australia 1969) all students underwent the routine Intelligence Quotient (IQ) test. It was designed to test how 'smart' we were and was used as a basis for class and level assignment/allocation. Fortunately, I was placed in the highest level for each subject — advanced — so in itself that was a great outcome. I don't recall now the exact IQ I was labelled with but I do remember its impact.

I recall that it was less than someone else I thought was pretty stupid in his behavior and quite cruel. I asked myself "How can he be more intelligent than me when he's always acting up and being nasty?"

What that IQ test did in my mind though (until many years later when I *dropped the external label/value and the internal barriers to achievement*) was label and box me as intelligent '*to a certain point*'. I was told that that was the intelligence level I would have for the rest of my life and worst part of all, I *believed* what I was told.

No amount of my mother's pressuring me to do better at school (even though I was studying at advanced level already!) made a difference to how I felt about that IQ number. The number stayed in my head for a long, long time. But once I let go of the number, I allowed myself to be who I was born to be, without someone else, or a test, telling me what I *wasn't* going to be.

In my second year of high school I was still hung up on the IQ number and was not doing very well in Advanced Science, even though I loved the subject. I wasn't able to get focused for some reason. That year I didn't even make a Pass, and I went down two levels to Ordinary level Science in my third year of high school (Form Three). Fortunately for me my Form Three teacher was a dead ringer for Michael Cole out of Mod Squad, whom I was desperately in love with (so I thought), and so I listened intently to everything he had to say.

But, it wasn't so much the fact that he was so good looking, it was more that he showed he really cared how well I did.

He kept challenging me to do better, but in a nice way. No ridicule, no punishment, just pure encouragement.

And the result?

Well, I sat for the Advanced level exam (from an Ordinary level seat of course) and came third out of the entire year of students.

I never saw him again after that, but I will never forget the priceless gift he gave me — belief in my ability to succeed.

CHAPTER 7
Mixed Messages and Mind Games

Mixed messages are very common in everyday dialogue. One person gives you one opinion, another person gives an opinion that's totally opposite. Your conscious mind processes each opinion and you form your own conclusion(s) in time. You make a choice what to believe and what to remember.

For example: you receive an instruction from a supervisor, and then they give you another instruction which appears to negate the first instruction or is in total contradiction with the expected outcome.

There are some logical conclusions that can be drawn: the *communicator* is confused, has simply changed their mind, is deliberately playing mind games (I'll illustrate this a little later), has forgotten the first instruction given, is under pressure and tells a lie in order to deflect scrutiny, or even time may have changed events therefore new ground rules apply.

Likewise, the *communicatee* may not have heard the instructions correctly (e.g. hearing a name when you said a location; hearing Friday when you said Monday), may be in a negative mindset, may simply not have heard you (i.e. not actively listening), may be under significant stress which in itself can create short-term memory loss and cause hearing dysfunction. Any number of reasons can be valid reasons.

The important thing to remember to do is to clarify understanding as early as possible.

Another example: One parent tells their 12 year old child they are very clever and one day will be able to do whatever they want to do. The other parent tells the child that achieving in life is not looked upon favourably, that nobody likes overly smart people, and that they'll never be good enough to make anything out of their life.

The child has just received completely opposite messages from the two most influential people in its life!

What is the child to do? How will he/she know what is true and fair?

Obviously the parent doing the putting down and 'boxing' of the child has their own grave feelings of inadequacy, is negatively programmed and is also in a negative mindset. The encouraging parent is positively programmed, is in a positive mindset, and is already winning at life and therefore easily able to help the child to realize their full potential.

Of course the most favorable situation for any child would be to live with parents who are both of the same positive mindset and internal programming! Then positive will perpetuate positive and generational change can easily occur.

Regardless of the circumstance, it is primarily the communicator's responsibility to ensure the message is understood by the communicatee, and to restate the communication as many times as the communicatee needs in order to understand the intent of the communication.

During this clarification period the communicatee should paraphrase what they heard and then both parties can identify the error in understanding and therefore resolve any confusion.

We are constantly receiving mixed messages every day — through the media and advertising, at work, at school, from our families, our friends, politicians, etc. There are subliminal messages in every aspect of life that can, if you choose, set boundaries and limitations around you.

How often do you read and hear that you will do or be a certain way because of your:
- gender
- age or generational group (e.g. Baby Boomer, Gen Y, Gen X, Millennial)
- astrological sign (Pisces, Libra etc.)
- personality type (A, B etc.)

- leadership style
- health status (e.g. labelled "disabled" when all you really have are human performance challenges)
- education level
- socio-economic status
- up-bringing
- height, weight, color
- nationality
- religion
- race
- Jungian preference; or even
- Myers-Briggs Type (MBTI)?

It is your choice whether to believe information you are fed or whether to discard it. Not everyone will communicate truth, so you must let your conscious mind process and validate the information to determine what is true and correct (as you know it). When you consciously make a decision to keep or discard information, your subconscious will follow suit.

To be *discerning* about the information you receive is the key to its effective utilization. Ascertain what information is valid and true, useful and constructive, and then apply it in a manner that achieves positive, worthwhile outcomes. There is so much we are fed each day that is blatantly misleading, untrue, unfounded and destructive. What long term benefit does misinformation serve? You have the power to discern what you hear and see.

YOU HAVE THE POWER TO DISCERN WHAT YOU HEAR AND SEE

By far, the most concerning aspect of communication is the mental confusion that can manifest as a result of the words that you use.

A mixed message and confused mindset example is:

In response to a question or statement you say "Yes No, that's . . . ."

Where on earth did "Yes No" come from? It's either 'Yes' or 'No', and even better still, don't use either word, ...
just start with "That's . . . . ".

A further example:

"I'm in two minds about this!"

My suggestion is that you *not* stay in "two minds" — make up one of them and stick with that.

We humans generally speak more words than we need to. We fill silence and tranquillity with empty words.
Do you know when you do that?
Let's look at one example................ a group of people is talking together, bonding in communication and then someone new comes into the group. The talk stops. The new person starts chatting to fill in the silence. Why? Do they want to be included?
The better solution would be for the new person to just sit down and wait for the group to start talking again. Of course, if there was still silence then that is the cue for the new person to leave. Obviously the conversation is not something the person is welcome to hear . . . .
Some of you will say that's very rude. Well, in fact it's not rude.
It's simply the group not allowing the new person to control the outcome for his/her benefit alone.

So what is so destructive about *mind games*?

Mind games are all about deceit. They are all about wanting total control over someone else and deliberately choosing conflicting or ambiguous statements to confuse.
One of the cruelest things a parent can do is deliberately play games with their children's heads and hearts. Playing favorites, constantly changing

your mind, inconsistent punishing or guidance, unfounded humiliation or ridicule, especially when done in public, is a sure fire way to damage or destroy your child's self-esteem, cause them mental confusion and thus pave the way for inconsistent and negative subconscious programming.

By doing this you are setting your child up for a long, hard struggle ahead *just* to clear the confusion from their mind. Is that what you are meant to be doing as a good parent?

Mind games practiced in business and social circles are most often done in an effort to gain control over others, manipulate a situation or outcome, disempower, deliberately cause confusion, deflect scrutiny, hide motives, and even to belittle.

So often I hear men admit to playing mind games so that women don't know what they have planned or what they are thinking. What is the sense in that? It is not open, transparent, honest and caring to deliberately mislead someone for your own benefit. That becomes a WIN/LOSE destructive outcome. And of course a woman will stay cautious and mistrusting if you demonstrate that behavior repeatedly.

What you must do is rise above the desire or temptation to hide things, have faith that telling the truth and being totally up front will achieve a WIN/WIN outcome, and then stick with that approach. Don't fall back into mind game mode. It won't win you any friends or respect; not in the long term.

In military operations for instance, mind games become an essential component of psychological warfare. Having the edge over the (perceived) enemy is an important margin to create when planning and executing a military campaign.

But remember, in everyday life we are not at war and the enemy is not all around us.

It is the use of mind games by those in everyday life, those who feel inadequate, weak, intimidated, insecure and unhappy, where the outcomes become the most grave.

Mind games are used by bullies. Mind games destroy team work, relationships, trust and respect. They are a significant cause of enduring mental illness for many people.

Mind games are therefore *not* a positive and constructive use of personal power.

No Boxing Allowed

CHAPTER 8

Growing Beyond Fear

What is fear?

Fear is a learned response to unknown stimuli. It is an emotion (often described as worry) of negative anticipation and is usually not founded in reality or fact.

There are many fears — fears of not coping, not being loved, falling, not succeeding, losing, ending, surviving, the unknown — too many to mention. Think back to when you last felt fearful. Was the fear justified and founded in something real? Was the outcome as severe as you had anticipated? Was the feeling of fear there because you hadn't gathered all the available information or logically assessed the risks associated? The more fact you have on which to base decisions, the more you trust your intuition, the less likely fear will find a home, and the more positive the outcome and energy is likely to be.

Worry thrives where negative energy abounds. Feeling worry and fear is like making a deposit into a bank that pays a negative return on your investment. You are putting emotional energy into something that hasn't happened yet. It may not happen, so why worry and be fearful?

DON'T PUT EMOTIONAL ENERGY INTO SOMETHING THAT HASN'T HAPPENED YET

So why are people fearful some times and not at other times? If there was one simple answer to this, we would already know.

Facing fears head on must be done in a controlled and considered way in order for the best possible outcome to result. Forcing yourself to work through fears just because other people don't share the same fear is not a good foundation.

If you fear snakes don't hide from them, but don't go looking for them either. Work to understand *why* you fear them first — that is the root cause that needs resolving, not just the symptoms of fear.

When you understand *why* you fear then you are best placed to work out whether the reasons are realistic and legitimate, or whether there is no logical foundation to keep living in fear.

So what happens inside when we feel fear — what are the symptoms?

We may begin to perspire, our heart may race, our thinking may become confused or distorted, our palms may become damp, we may become breathless, our limbs shake, our throat may feel like the stomach has jumped up to join it.

Any number of nervous system responses may prevail. Recognizing and controlling these feelings and responses is therefore critical to harnessing the negative power that is created by fear. Fear creates a negative energy in the body. It disturbs tranquillity and inner calm. Identifying the root cause of fear can be achieved in the same manner as mentioned in Part 1, Chapter 4. Once you know and understand why you fear, you are best placed to rationalize the fear and remove it, permanently.

In the next two chapters I talk about accelerated ways of achieving inner understanding and change. Change, regardless of how it is facilitated, must be done at a manageable pace otherwise inner calm is disturbed. Pushing too quickly to heal can actually create or perpetuate pain.

Given that a fear response generates a lowered level of personal control over a sequence of events, the most inappropriate action you can take is to *project* your fear onto others, particularly children or those to whom your care, support and guidance is entrusted. They are the most vulnerable. People will learn from and imitate a fear response, *especially* if its negative energy is radiated out by a person of enormous personal power. Often times the person in fear may not know the level of energy they are radiating. If you recognize in yourself when this is happening, when you are radiating negative, uncontrolled energy, discretely move away from the people you are with. Get out of their personal 'energy' space.

By backing away you can radiate the negative energy into the wider universal space and not have such a direct impact on the people around you. Your negative energy will still be out there, but the positive energy created by those who do not feel fear, will automatically diffuse and disempower the negative energy you created.

A simple example of this is where you are in a threatening situation, say confronted by a would-be attacker. It is perfectly normal for you to want to fight or flee — that is the autonomic nervous system doing all the right things to protect you.

What doesn't need to occur though, is a fear response. In fear, you are not in full control.

When you are confronted by an attacker you need to be in full control, so it's best to harness the fear response very quickly and channel that negative energy in a way that is self-protective not destructive i.e. use the negative reaction to your advantage, to channel positive power in your self-defense.

When I decided to end a long marriage many years ago I had, some six years prior to that, decided I didn't want to be in the marriage anymore. I was not getting what I needed and decided that I was better to build a life with someone else than be unhappy stuck in a non-nurturing marriage.

Circumstances changed though when my (then) husband suffered several heart episodes, including a heart attack at home. He subsequently required surgery, had a cardiac arrest post-operatively but recovered enough to be able to return to work.

Initially I saw this as an opportunity to start over, encouraging him to talk about his experience and his concerns, to heal himself of the painful baggage he had carried for decades, and perhaps save our marriage. But after six months of little communication and no improvement in his approach to me and the world, I saw my long term role as just his nurse and minder. I therefore began grieving knowing that one day, when I felt the time was right, I'd leave with no fear of the future and what it would hold.

I didn't want to leave whilst our son was not old enough to understand, nor did I want to leave until I'd healed myself of all the pain associated with the marriage. That was my choice and I knew I wanted to be leaving for all the right reasons, not just a knee-jerk reaction to something else. It took nearly five years for the grieving process to complete. I still felt a sense of caring and compassion for him at the time, but there was no love as I had felt before.

When you can achieve a memory recall as I have just done, without fear attached to the memory, or any kind of pain, then you know you have fully healed.

These days I recover and heal much more quickly from painful events given that my mind is uncluttered. In times past I used self-hypnosis to heal, and whilst I think very highly of this technique to facilitate healing and change, and it's an excellent method to face and erase fears, change that occurs too quickly can have a major negative impact on you. You *must* manage change at a rate that does not cause more pain. Pain is the body's last sign that something is wrong. To ignore the signal of pain is very foolish.

In the next chapter I'll explain more about hypnosis and hypnotherapy, but suffice to say that where some fears are built up over time or are the result of what people tell you, and/or what you experience, you can heal yourself of fears much more quickly if your physical health is at a premium level. In my case, my mind has always worked at lightning speed and the older I get the more I place emphasis on nurturing the brain. Yes, it is only one essential organ of the body but without it functioning at a premium and being fed all the right nutrients every day, thought processes (both conscious and subconscious) will not occur in the best way possible and the rest of the body will not receive the messages it needs to do what it is built to do.

I mentioned earlier that while there is still emotional pain attached to a memory (and fear is associated with the memory) then you are *more likely* to continue to feel a fear response each time you have a memory recall. The painful feelings attached to memories heal at different rates and your mind and heart will work through *which* feelings can be healed ahead of others. In essence what I'm saying is that through the process of healing, feelings will change. Some pain will go quite quickly whereas other pain may linger as long as you are holding on to the memory, instead of letting go what is not needed.

The mere act of acknowledging that you no longer wish to feel the pain, saying out loud "I don't want to hurt anymore" will set a course to the future and you will have begun to let go. You will have begun to heal. Likewise, until you address the fear aspect, that will continue to surface as well. Understanding why you still feel fearful is an important step in that journey.

No Boxing Allowed

CHAPTER 9

Letting Go Of The Baggage

How many times have you heard someone say "Everyone carries baggage" or "Everyone has their issues"? Personally I've lost count and each time (where the risk level is not extreme) I challenge the statement with "No they don't."

Not everyone carries baggage; not everyone has issues. A negative mindset person will say those things, because that is the basis they are working from and that's their excuse for holding onto 'stuff' unnecessarily.

Baggage is simply the emotional pain[7] associated with a memory. At any point in time you may be burdened with a level of pain, however it is *your* choice whether to hold onto the baggage or let it go. It is *your* choice whether you achieve closure on things of the past or continue to foster negative and painful thought processes.

The speed at which someone lets go of their emotional pain is directly related to their mindset, internal programming, desire to be free of emotional burdens, instinctive self-protection[8] and their general physical health (which will influence the speed at which synapses occur and thus the speed at which the subconscious mind can process memories and their emotional links).

---

[7] As distinct from disappointment.

[8] i.e. some painful memories are important to retain, as it is from these that we can learn not to repeat the same mistakes. The pain, though, does *not* have to be retained.

No two people will be the same in how they process and recover from painful events.

Talking through issues with someone you trust and in whom you have confidence, is a terrific way to lessen the burden on yourself. You can choose a health practitioner, counsellor, friend, or family member to talk to, for example, but what is most important is not to *dump* your stuff on that person. Off-loading emotional pain can be done in a way that is constructive for both parties. Dumping is destructive — the receiver becomes flooded with *your* stuff and that is not fair or justifiable.

We all know those people (let's call them "dumpers") who look for the positive one in the crowd — they are feeling so bad they need to dump their stuff el pronto. They ease in with some general conversation and when they sense the receiver is feeling strong enough to handle the full load, they dump.

Of course, once the dumpers have off-loaded they feel fantastic and the receiver of the load feels heavier and less positive than before. A WIN/ LOSE scenario has just played out.

Would the receiver openly seek out the dumper and ask for a second dose? I doubt it.

Luckily for the receiver, they can usually bounce back quickly, they are positively programmed; they off-load their own baggage in selfless ways, gently, caringly. The dumper on the other hand is busily loading up all over again with more, and often times the *same*, pain baggage. The dumpers are getting ready to dump on the next positive person they come across.

So the cycle continues.

Your responsibility is, firstly, to acknowledge that the emotional pain you may be feeling is not something that requires a permanent home in your mind, and secondly, to activate ways of removing the baggage *permanently* from your mind.

When people are screaming at one another or hurting in other ways, they are expressing their pain. Pain about what? Only they know and only they can find the permanent remedy.

DON'T BE A DUMPER – LEARN TO HEAL YOURSELF OF THE PAIN YOU CARRY

Professional counselling can be an effective way to work through chronic and intense emotional pain, and eliminate it. However you must *want,* and make a conscious decision, to remove the pain permanently in order for that to happen.

Hypnosis, either facilitated by a qualified and experienced practitioner or self-practiced, is a fast and effective method for achieving inner healing and serenity. The various forms of meditation are also amazingly effective in securing inner peace and calm. Whatever works successfully for you is the best solution.

Every day we see the baggage carried by one person, a family, a community, a religion and even a country, destroy goodwill and relationships somewhere in the world. Is that the kind of world we want to have?

Most people talk about how nice it would be to have peace in the world. What I put to you is, when everyone wants peace (without doubt), is prepared to heal themselves of their emotional pain and forget all about needing or wanting to have control over others, then we *will* achieve peace.

When the majority of the world's people take a step forward to inner tranquillity, the world will follow suit. *That* is the unique power we human beings have to give to each other and to our earth – the power of choice and belief in a positive outcome.

What causes war? Well, at a simplistic and human emotion-based level it is any number of negative energy things – the desire for control, power over others, greed, fear, revenge, pain and so on.

When we think about wars that have gone on for centuries we have to look at *generational baggage* as being a major root cause i.e. baggage passed down through generations of people. Generational baggage is not something unique to war fighting between nations. It is as common in dysfunctional families (families where a rot has set in) as it is in religions, political movements, organizations, cults and close communities.

Generation after generation repeating the same mistakes, not healing from pain, not letting go of the past.

For example, families perpetuating violence through the generations. So your mother beat you! So your father yelled at you! Does that mean you must beat on or yell at your own children? Of course it doesn't.

Organizations (especially those involved in military and law enforcement operations) allowing old scars and pain to taint and influence future direction. Their employees not letting go of things past and thus allowing the organization to grow and change for the better. The "things are just fine the way they are" type scenario is perpetuated.

All our actions are a choice. We choose to be ugly toward one another, or we choose to be nice. It's really as simple as that.

Treating generational baggage the same as any other dis-ease is an excellent start. Find out the root cause(s), determine strategies to eliminate those cause(s), and hold very strong in not allowing symptoms to re-surface.

———⁓⁓⁓∽○◯◉○◉◯∽⁓⁓⁓———

Your home is a sacred place, your sanctuary. Do you really want to dump your baggage on those you love? Make them suffer for the pain you carry? Any loving person would think not.

Likewise, is someone else's home the place to dump your baggage?

"You hurt the ones you love the most" are words spoken by a baggage-ridden person who has no consideration for the feelings of others. In your relationships with others do you say things deliberately to hurt; things that are designed to belittle or ridicule? The only reason you would choose to do that is to vent your baggage on someone else and cause them pain. A grave mistake in the universal justice sense.

A perfect example: You've been married for 40 years; you're both looking a little different than you did when you were younger. Intimacy between you is limited and therefore you may be feeling frustrated and unloved. What do you do to resolve this?

Well, in *Scenario One* you could make cutting remarks at each other about how one part of the anatomy is not as firm as it used to be, or speak of each other in condemning and condescending terms when you talk to other people.

Alternately, in *Scenario Two* you could sit down together, gently and openly explain the pain you are feeling, and why you feel that way, find common ground to work from and then come up with an action plan to reverse the trend.

Scenario One is the path most couples choose, mainly out of fear in baring their inner most thoughts. After 40 years of marriage you should certainly be able to talk honestly with one another, shouldn't you?

Scenario Two on the other hand is one that requires admitting that something isn't quite right inside yourself, that you're not truly tranquil and calm. That's a challenging place for many people to get to, but until you *can* journey there (either on your own or facilitated by a professional) the less likely Scenario Two will become your first choice, every time.

As the home is no place to dump your baggage, likewise the workplace is no place to dump your baggage either — especially so when someone new comes into the area. They have a job to do and that job does not include being the new psychologist or counsellor receiving your baggage at every corner. I've often wondered why people come to work and offload.

In 2004 one young work colleague said to me "You always come to work happy. You never have anything to offload like other people." At the time I found that amazing because any kind of pain is personal and I was in a place of business, not my private sanctum. I also wondered why so many people think they have the right to come to work and offload. Why have we allowed that to become the norm? Why have we not stood up and said, as a holistic group, **"Welcome to work, but leave your baggage at the door thanks!"**?

Work is also not the place to show the world you are currently burdened with baggage — yelling, getting angry, swearing, getting huffy, sulking, bullying, teasing, scaring, huffing and puffing, crying all the time etc. — these are all signs of baggage overload.

Take the male work associate you heard of earlier — he huffed and puffed, exhaled loudly, talked to fill quiet time, shoved things, made wise cracks or sexist remarks, grunted loudly, paced up and down the corridor — he put negative energy out into the universe with every breath and with every step. He used these means to offload his stuff.

Yes, he's likely in need of professional support to gain emotional release — but importantly, he needs to learn to vent his feelings in a controlled and structured way. Going into another room, or outside, and venting his angers, frustrations and pain alone into the universe is a much less destructive way to let go than pushing his pain onto the people around him in the office.

Having respite or time out, what some people call a mental health day, is critical to being able to function respectfully and caringly towards other people in the workplace. The more employees who actively care for the wellbeing of others around them, the more actively caring the organization will become. There will be less incidents resulting in injury and illness, there will be less harassment and bullying, and there will be more harmony and trust between everyone.

Truly Great Leaders will keep good control of any emotional pain they may be feeling, will carry on their work and present themselves to the world as best as they can as if nothing is wrong. They won't *dump* their stuff on other people every day. They will be available to listen to others, rather than feel the need to always speak. They know the true value of two ears and one mouth — the value of twice as much listening as talking.

LISTEN TWICE AS MUCH AS YOU SPEAK

I will make a very special point here about positive energy *suckers*. I talked of dumpers before but suckers can, and often are, far more destructive. You learned that the negative, baggage ridden dumpers look for someone super positive so that they can dump their load. Well the same negative, baggage-ridden people may not be looking to dump, they may be looking to insert their emotional catheter into you and get a quick hit.

Protecting yourself from suckers and managing how fast you heal from pain is vitally important. Here is why:

In early 2002 (just before I turned 45) I reached the point where I was feeling like a sponge fully soaked. I'd cared for, nurtured, listened to, motivated, encouraged and held other people up *all* my life. To the most part I was worn out, especially because I was doing all this for myself as well.

I decided to rid myself of my remaining fears and the baggage I knew I was carrying — all the pain associated with other people in my life who had had a negative impact. By my choice and under my own strong motivation, I undertook a short series of hypnotherapy sessions.

After approximately 8 hours over a very rapid 3 weeks I felt like a whole new person. What I didn't realize however was that, at the spiritual and universal energy levels, I really was reborn.

I also found out a year later, when I gained qualifications in clinical hypnotherapy myself, that 'best practice' in hypnotherapy is to allow weeks or months between sessions. I had therefore really pushed the envelope of mental and emotional strength to undergo what I had in such a short time.

The good news is that what I experienced during those sessions can only be described as mind cleansing — it was *emotional exfoliation* at the deepest possible level. I felt *no* pain; I felt *no* fear; I loved *everyone*; I saw *everyone* as a friend and ally — even strangers in the street.

On the flipside though, I had inadvertently been stripped of *every* defense mechanism I'd ever used for survival. My mind was overriding the autonomic nervous system — the fight-flight reflex wasn't working properly. Things that would terrify the strongest of people I was immune and completely unresponsive to. Memories of painful events couldn't be recalled. After all, that is what I'd wanted to achieve under hypnosis and unfortunately the facilitator of my hypnosis didn't know just how strong my mind was in achieving an outcome.

The dynamics of my personal and business relationships changed dramatically and very quickly. I wanted to give all the wonderful energy I could channel (using the Reiki technique) to *everyone* around me. The almost fatal mistake I made though was to forget to give to myself, to nurture and care for myself.

I fell victim to every dumper and sucker in my vicinity. People wanted loads of time with me, they wanted my healing hands on them; they wanted to get in my personal space (in my aura).

For the first 6 months my mind seemed like a blank tape, as I described to you in Chapter 6. I trusted everyone so I confided in friends I thought I knew well (in hindsight a huge mistake!). Everything people told me I believed — I believed everyone spoke the truth like me, so why not believe what they say? I didn't have any memory to recall otherwise, so how was I to know that they were deliberately feeding me lies and rubbish?

Very rapidly I was back in the real world and realized how vulnerable I was to being used, robbed, abused, intimidated and manipulated. My home was broken into during this time and a large quantity of valuable things taken. My trusted neighbors were later discovered to be the perpetrators.

After 9 months I needed another major emotional exfoliation. I'd literally taken on and was weighed down by everyone else's stuff and could no longer find myself and gain a sense of tranquillity in amongst all that. I did not have an adequate defense shield established.

However, through the care of my loving family, holding inside myself the deep love I have for my son, respite away from everyone toxic and a few months of solid inner healing, I was able to strengthen and return to the real world once again. That was in early 2003.

Negative, toxic people presented huge challenges for me over the next 3 years; I avoided them like the plague or held them at arms' distance.

I'm thankful that with my very strong mind, the will to overcome all adversity and the unwavering determination to restore myself to what I called normality, I've been very successful in achieving the outcome I set. I learned how to really channel nurturing universal energy to myself, far beyond the teachings of my Reiki Master, to build up and maintain an invisible barrier for protection. A white shield that allows me to feel, very quickly, when there is negative energy being emitted by someone.

The memories that could assist in my future defense became recallable as before, but I do not hold any pain associated. I thank God that I had the benefit of time to achieve this level of self-protection, to achieve a profound self awareness. And to this day (2016) I no longer need to use self-hypnosis to heal. The serenity I achieve through relaxation, clearing my mind, and maintaining positive inner dialogue nurtures me at a cellular level every day, all day.

What I say to you is — be *thankful* for the memories that you have as they are the key to your future health and wellbeing. Have faith that the memories you no longer need *will* be erased in time and have confidence that, with strong inner resolve, you *will* heal yourself from any emotional pain that you carry.

CHAPTER 10

Using Personal Power to Re-engineer Your Thinking and Re-program Your Mind To The Positive

In the previous chapter we explored emotional pain and the baggage most people choose to carry. In earlier chapters we looked at mindsets, internal programming and how you have the power of choice in everything you do and say.

If you have, by this stage, identified that your mindset is usually negative, then what is offered in this chapter is a cost free and life changing opportunity – to re-discover and harness positivity.

At some stage whilst reading this book you may have acknowledged that there is something not quite in sync within yourself, your essence is not resonating well or something may not feel at ease.

Perhaps you don't like the dialogue you use, the way you treat people, the way you accept the treatment of others, your behavior or attitudes.

Perhaps you've been making the wrong moral choices and the universe is delivering signs for you to re-evaluate how and why you're doing things.

When you've decided to make a change, remember change is always an opportunity *never* a threat. When you don't know what the change will actually bring because it represents a *future* event that hasn't occurred yet, to believe change is a threat then you're well and truly stuck in a negative mindset.

CHANGE IS ALWAYS AN OPPORTUNITY, NEVER A THREAT

So how do you change your mindset from negative to positive and keep it that way?

- Firstly, you need to have undertaken the self-exploration, self-awareness and *emotional exfoliation* activities talked about in earlier chapters.
- Secondly, you must accept that the change process, once started, is not to stop. You must not revert back to your old ways.
- And thirdly, you must maintain a high level of self-motivation.

Don't look to others to motivate you. Others can inspire you, but the strongest and most sustainable motivation comes from within.

THE MOST SUSTAINABLE MOTIVATION COMES FROM WITHIN

Make no mistake, re-programming your subconscious and re-engineering your thinking is very hard work. It requires cleaning out the negative, letting go of the baggage and sustained effort in order to realize all the benefits.

Granted, it's far easier to send and receive negative messages. Our current society is full of negative dialogue and messages, both direct and subliminal. So it takes courage, consistency, and the mental alertness to switch off to and/or erase negative messages received from within yourself and from others.

No-one is perfect. Everyone has their ups and downs. The key to personal power, in this sense, is recognizing what's happening within you, nurturing the thoughts and feelings that are constructive for you and others, going with the flow of change, and switching off the negative thoughts and feelings that are destructive.

Yes, some of you will say "a little bit of negativity brings you back to reality". Being told something you don't want to hear is certainly a negative experience.

What you should do firstly is verify that what you've been told is true and then, secondly, work within yourself to heal from the pain of the new truth you've learned.

Some people can quite easily journey through life being utterly miserable. What I want you to question within yourself is what goodness comes from continual doses of negativity. How does it make you feel? Lively and supported? I'd think not.

Like you, I know people who *thrive* on negativity. If someone isn't dying, suffering, hurt or sick their day isn't complete and fulfilled. They feed on other people's woes. They live for the worst case scenario to happen. And, as a consequence, aren't they usually pretty morbid to be around for long?

There's no doubt that with some diagnosed mental and physical illnesses and emotional states of mind there's little to be done to counter the negativity that some people feel. Some don't even recognize how negative they are, the negativity often compounded by medication. The challenge here is to find a level of tolerance within yourself, so that you can interact with negative people but yet not allow *their* state of mind and emotion to negatively impact on *you*.

Changing from having a negative mindset to having a positive mindset is something you need to work on every day, every hour, every minute, every second. After all, you are re-programming your subconscious mind to a whole new way of receiving, processing and producing messages.

When someone asks you how you are, say "Fantastic", "Great", "Terrific", "Outstanding", "Very well, thank you". Use positive, empowering words that truly express how you *want to* or (actually) do feel.

If you're genuinely feeling off or unwell one day, give a positively-oriented response like "Not as well as usual, but getting better, thank you."

Keep yourself focused on the positive at all times and *always* speak the truth. There is no gain to be made in lying. When you lie you're lying to yourself first, feeding and growing negative energy inside, and then projecting it out onto others.

If you hear yourself slipping back to the old ways, such as "Oh, not too bad", "Oh, all right", "Could be better", give yourself a prod.

Immediately correct the negative phrase with a motivating phrase. Keep repeating to yourself "I am feeling better now", "I'll be much better tomorrow" and *believe it.*

THE SECRET TO SUCCESSFUL RE-PROGRAMMING IS BELIEVING

Positive communication from others and from within will, if consistently processed and applied, beget more positive.

It doesn't take much to alter a computer program to perform a new function or do an old function differently. Your brain is really just like a super-powerful computer, so why not trust in your ability to make permanent changes to it?

It's all a matter of choice.

Since first seeding the idea of this book, I've wondered many times if someone might use this information to achieve a negative outcome. Well, the answer to that is yes.

If someone chooses to be more negative than before, chooses to change to become destructive and cruel, then that's exactly the outcome that will be achieved (each step that we take, each decision we make has a strategic impact).

I'm sure you will have come to realize though that the karmic outcome for that person and their soul will not be the same as someone who chooses to change to the positive.

Good will overcome evil every time. That is a universal justice law that no human being has the power to alter. It is beyond all of us.

Those who have made the journey to positivity will always choose to stay there, rather than allow themselves to be sucked back to the dark place that negativity represents and brings.

No Boxing Allowed

PART 2

The Constructive Use of Personal Power

CHAPTER 1

Positive and Negative Applications of Power

The person you said hello to in the street or smiled at the other day, or the one who smiled at you, has changed your life forever.

NEVER UNDERESTIMATE THE POSITIVE POWER OF A SMILE

Think of times when you have felt like no-one loved you, the world was ganging up on you, or that no-one cared. Then along comes a smile from a complete stranger or someone you haven't seen in ages. Did you receive that smile with gratitude? With a positive response, like a reciprocal smile or a simple acknowledgment? Or did you respond with disbelief or cynicism, thinking "Why smile at me?; what do you want?; why are you so happy?"

Nearly every day I witness the unjustified criticism or belittling of one human by another. What purpose is served by doing this? Is it one person's attempt to make the other behave differently, be different to what they are, fit the 'box' that's been picked out for them? What right do humans have to unjustly criticize others when they are not perfect themselves? What right do humans have to *be* mean and cruel to others, just because they *feel* like being mean and cruel?

The negative karmic energy humans emit when they are being controlling, critical, mean, cruel, jealous, angry, deceitful, sarcastic, egotistical, self-righteous or violent is profound, yet to most people this negative energy is not felt beyond the moment.

The negative karmic energy that snobbishness, selfishness, arrogance, ambiguity, racism and presumption put way out into the wider universe can never be taken back. Negative energies will seek to disrupt good energies and will cause significant negative stress responses in humans, plants and animals. Think about that for a minute.

The negative energy created by attack and counter-attack (given that an attack is usually founded in fear, the need for power and control over others, retaliation, hatred, vengeance etc.) is so toxic for the human race, our earth and the universe, its strategic impact cannot even be measured.

The positive karmic energy that humans emit when they're being loving, caring, considerate, kind, happy, truthful, complimentary, or gracious however, is even more profound. The positive energy will stay around the person radiating it. It will slowly and carefully radiate through everything it comes in contact with creating harmony, tranquillity, happiness and serenity. It will gather momentum and force with each further encounter of positive energy. It won't be destroyed by negative karmic energy. It will remain steadfast and strong against any negative it encounters.

If every single human on the face of this earth suddenly got angry or yelled in frustration, how much negative energy would be circulating around us all? On the other hand, if every human being suddenly radiated warmth and love out into the universe, how would that feel? It doesn't take a scientist to work out which one has the more constructive and enduring positive after-effect.

There are many deeply spiritual humans who know the gift of feeling another's energy the instant they come within a reasonable distance of each other. Some highly tuned humans even feel energies over vast distances. If someone is putting out negative karma, a spiritually receptive person will feel those energies without having to get within the negative person's karmic space or aura i.e. their personal space. The same principal applies for those emitting positive karma.

The important thing to remember about karma is that it *does* exist. A negative karma put out by you will come back and hit you square between the eyes, in your third eye or intuitive chakra zone. It may take seconds, minutes, weeks, months, years or, in the case of a major spiritual deficit, even another lifetime beyond your own. But, the negative karma *will* come back.

ALL KARMA COMES BACK

The other thing about negative karma is that it will come back *double in intensity each time.* The universe will decide when and how your soul's lesson is best learned and then the negative karma, double-fold from before, will be dealt to you to suffer through and learn from. If you don't understand the lesson the first time and correct your actions and words, the negative will be doubled again and then you will receive it back. The karmic lessons continue like this until your soul learns the lessons it has not yet learned in times past. Your soul will continue to learn lessons through lifetimes until it reaches its final destination of purity, clarity and perfection.

When you 'vent' your feelings into the wider universe — i.e. talk out loud and say how you really feel — if the universe believes that what you are saying needs to be channelled to the wrong-doer in the form of a lesson, then it will be. Universal justice will prevail. That is not to say that all negative things that happen to or around you are your *fault.* Sometimes the universe will decide when you need to work through disappointments and obstacles to achieve a better outcome. You may need to build strength this way, or be taught patience, be shown truth, be given time for reflection and readjustment of your strategic life plan.

The reasons for the karmic lessons may not be 'visible', in the intuitive sense, to you at the time.

If you really want it to though, time will certainly uncover the root causes for the karmic lessons and a greater understanding will be achieved.

Whilst a negative karma is returned double in intensity each time, a *positive karma will come back tenfold* what you put out. If you willingly and unselfishly donate $2, you will receive $20 some other way as soon afterwards as the universe believes you deserve it. If you smile at one person, 10 people will smile at you. If you give to another, 10 people will give to you. When you speak only truth, then truth will come back to you tenfold. People will honor you in ways you never thought imaginable.

Often times the way you receive is not noticeable at first, but if you focus on radiating positive karma, what you'll also learn to do is recognize the positive karma coming back to you. The more you put out the more you will want to put out, because it feels just fantastic to get positive karma back.

POSITIVE KARMA WILL COME BACK TO YOU TENFOLD

Harnessing and channelling your personal power – feeling it generating and building force inside, understanding these sensations created in the body and then projecting the power in a positive, calm, constructive and selfless way – is as important as eating, drinking and breathing. If used in inappropriate ways, irrecoverable damage can be done to relationships, families, communities, countries, the world and the universe.

If you accuse without just cause, the repercussions can be catastrophic. If you stop listening, the ones you really need the most will stop talking to you. If you repeatedly reject someone because you think you are helping them to build character, they will leave you in every way possible, eventually.

Rejection does not build character. It simply delivers the message – I don't want you around. Listen to the messages you are given and then act on your intuition.

A younger friend I knew a decade ago ruled her family with an iron fist. What she wanted always came first. She put her own needs and desires well above others. She spent money on superficial things (e.g. hundreds of shoes). When I asked her whether controlling other people was important to her sense of security and her ability to deal with anxiety attacks she said "I don't control my friends, but I do control my family."

Interestingly, she carried a huge amount of baggage — expressed as anger outbursts, caustic criticism, frequent swearing, rejection and abuse of others. Yet, when her positivity was flowing she was the complete opposite — caring, considerate and complimentary.

She openly admitted learning from me to look for the goodness in others instead of always looking for the bad. That became her way of staying positive through what she perceived as a negative existence.

I don't know to this day if her positivity overcame the negative. She kept changing her mind and lacked motivation back then — two signs that there wasn't likely to be a permanent change for the better.

Remember that having control of your own destiny is vital to achieving stability and inner tranquillity. However, taking control of *yourself* is the key, not seeking control over *others*.

If you're on the lookout, I'm sure that every day you will witness one person's attempts/success at controlling another.

With the exception of those mentioned in the footnote of the Introduction, no adult has the right to control another adult. You can inspire, lead, influence, persuade and convince, but the second you attempt to actually control a person or dictate, you are using your personal power in a destructive and negative way.

TAKE CONTROL OF YOURSELF, NOT OTHERS

Some specific examples of the positive and negative use of personal power are provided below to help you in your understanding of how critical choice is, in our relationships with others:

Positive Personal Power:
- Kindness, caring, compassion and consideration
- Giving people some of your time
- Helping others to WIN in life
- Respecting another's privacy and time
- Actively listening
- Truthfulness and complete integrity in all that you do and say
- Transparency and openness
- Being accurate and factual, not presumptuous
- Asking questions to further understanding and/or seek clarity
- Following through on promises where humanly possible and justified
- Taking time and giving people time to make important decisions
- Giving people enough time to heal, to perform at their best and deliver mutually-beneficial outcomes
- Saying sorry when you do something wrong or inconvenience someone

Negative Personal Power:
- Displaying disrespect, aloofness or rudeness
- Playing mind games and deliberately giving mixed messages
- Being a snob
- Stalking, voyeurism
- Bullying, harassment, ridicule, stand-over tactics
- Talking over people or bombarding them with questions
- Being loud when all others around you are being quiet e.g. coming into a quiet television or reading zone and talking over what's being absorbed by the listeners
- Forcing your sexuality onto someone
- Repeated and frequent attempts to have another person notice you e.g. looking at them all the time, walking past them, creating unnecessary conversation
- Being antagonistic
- Interrupting before someone is finished speaking
- Refuting everything someone says without due cause
  - Withholding information that is critical to the empowerment of others
  - Pushing hard for something to happen[9]

---

[9] see Part 3, Chapter 3

- Impatience
- Categorizing and boxing people based on gender e.g. "All women are moody", "That's typical of a man"
- Selfish behavior on the road e.g. tail-gating, blocking, cutting in
- Pushing to perform a task when you're ready, not when it's the best time for your team
- Repeating an opinion over and over in a public forum with the objective of converting everyone to your opinion
- Disregard for people, or pushing people to work, when they're unwell or ill
- Making others work harder than yourself
- Feigning a difficulty or illness e.g. crying wolf
- Exaggerating fact(s) to gain more support
- Threatening a punishment in an attempt to control another's actions or words e.g. "I'll divorce you if you grow a moustache"
- Seeking to control another adult and restrict their growth e.g. "I like you just the way you are, don't ever change"
- Any violent act against another human being e.g. murder, rape, assault, terrorism in all its forms, kidnapping or holding against someone's will, assassination
- Misrepresenting someone or something deliberately to gain a personal benefit
- Starting or perpetuating rumours
- Pretence or other attention-seeking behaviour

Wanting to have control over others is all about being insecure about your own personal power and how to use it. It will complicate your life in innumerable ways. With complications comes confusion, congestion, pain and apathy. Is that the kind of life you want for yourself and others around you?

Once you understand just how positively powerful you can be, you won't *ever* look to have control over other adults, or strive to have more power than someone else. You will feel comfortable just the way you are. Your motivations in life will change. You will value the simplicity of life.

No Boxing Allowed

CHAPTER 2

The Virtues of Great Leadership

Having leadership ability is all about giving quality guidance, direction, support and advice. Leaders have the innate ability to inspire others without even knowing they're doing it. Leaders aren't just the ones we see on the television, in the newspaper, in a glossy magazine. Leaders are all around us, quietly getting on with achieving, without fuss and bother, without loud acclamations.

My observations of and research into human leadership traits began before the age of 8. At that time I'd decided I wanted to be a published author and so my journey of discovery about what characterized Great Leaders began. I wanted to differentiate mainstream leaders from people who are truly strides ahead of others.

So, over the 4+ decades that followed I observed and learned from those around me, I developed my own leadership style beyond the mainstream, a style that resonated well for me, and I actively mentored and taught others to recognize and use their leadership abilities, whilst opening them up to the step beyond simply "leadership".

So what are the characteristics of Great Leaders in life? Well, quite simply they:

- seek the views of others, regardless of level or positional power

- empower others with relevant information[10]
- are not intimidated by anyone or anything
- are not racist and prejudiced
- walk the talk, consistently
- never just promise, they act
- never abuse their position of power or authority
- build and nurture relationships, not erode or destroy them with innuendo, gossip and lies
- demonstrate by actions, not just by words, that people are the most important asset on earth
- demonstrate care for people's health, safety and wellbeing
- when leading organizations, have people policies in place that reflect and ensure that an honest, communicative, safe, caring and just culture is the solid foundation for the organization
- actively listen, all the time
- are transparent and honest in all their dealings
- are consistently courteous, gracious, responsive and humble
- never hold grudges
- provide clear direction
- foster leadership and management ability in others
- mentor others without seeking tangible reward
- have a well thought out and robust vision
- can visualize an outcome
- remember people, their names and their contribution, next week, next month, next year, and the years after that — they never forget the positive things done by others
- empower others to have a say, to stand up for any perceived injustice, challenge and query decisions made
- reward and honor others in suitable ways — privately and publicly
- welcome others back if they decide leaving wasn't such a good idea
- rejoice when others activate personal choices that allow them to fulfil their chosen destiny
- always acknowledge and thank the *whole* team when a team outcome is achieved
- have an 'open door' policy that is not based on any hierarchical structure

---

[10] They *never* withhold information out of a fear of loss of their own power or to deliberately disempower or disadvantage another person

- stay positive, through even the worst adversity
- forgive
- stay focused on long term outcomes for the good of all humans
- never seek an outcome for themselves alone — they don't have an "It's all about me" attitude or push a purely personal agenda
- make decisions and stick with them
- never ridicule, bully, harass, or admonish another
- never lie
- rarely swear, if at all
- don't allow strategies and decision-making to be founded on or driven by personalities
- don't hide behind irony talk and sarcasm
- say sorry when they realize they have done something wrong
- make sure they are well prepared, but if necessary, freely and openly admit they don't know an answer if that is the case, and then seek out the answer and share it.

In any organization that employs people it's critical for the supervisors, managers and leaders to know that an employee's outputs and outcomes are only within the *employee's control*, not the employer's. The employer is there to inspire employees to follow direction and demonstrate loyalty. They should never force someone to do something against their will.

The difficulty arises in organizations that have a mission that involves keeping peace or upholding standards and rules i.e. command and control organizations such as defense and police. In these organizations legislation plays a big part in determining levels of power and control.

In Part 3 you will learn about how employees in command and control organizations can grow to become even more effective, and less destructive, in their use of positional and personal power.

As highlighted earlier, the most powerful and sustainable motivation lies within, and seeking to control others is a negative use of personal power.

So what must supervisors do differently?

They must learn ways to inspire team members, build confidence within their teams, negotiate for outcomes, and celebrate successes. Celebrating a successful outcome is *vital* to sustaining the positive energy as long into the future as possible.

CHAPTER 3

Leaders: Born or Made?

Using the premise that the majority of humans are born positively programmed, it is reasonable to conclude that the majority of humans therefore have the ability to inspire others — one of the characteristics of leadership. In that respect then, leaders could be seen as born rather than made.

There are those however who are born into and are raised in a negative environment, but who seek positive at every corner of life. They consciously fine-tune their leadership abilities throughout life and are, thus, self-made leaders who strive to better themselves at every opportunity. Through sheer hard work they eventually reach the point of calm inner resonance and at this point they will know, deep inside, that they have come into their own.

What I described in the previous chapter were the characteristics of Great Leaders — those whose leadership skills are so well honed they demonstrate the characteristics without any real effort. Being a Great Leader is second nature to them. They don't wake up in the morning and say, "Today I'll be great." They just *are*.

I have heard many people say "Leaders are born; you either have it or you don't". This appears to be a common theme in command-and-control organizations where promotion to higher ranks is equated to success. The very notion of being a leader at the bottom-most rank has been a foreign idea until recently.

Only now are we seeing military and other highly bureaucratic organizations understand that *leaders exist at every level.* Leadership is not about power. Leadership is about vision and inspiration.

To have a leader Corporal or a leader Midshipman is a far safer and more effective outcome than to say that leadership is reserved for the Generals and the Admirals.

Everyone is entitled to their opinion about leadership. What I put to you is that those who doubt your ability to grow your leadership skills are really saying that in order to be called a leader you have to:
- have achieved a high level in an organization
- be acclaimed by the masses
- be famous; or
- look different.

Rightly so, this is not correct.

Truly Great Leaders in life, whether born or made, have a positive personal power that is often described as charismatic. They have an illustrious quality about them. They are attractive, not in the beauty sense, in the energy sense. Their very presence brings lightness, positivity and joy to life. Their generosity and forgiveness is consistent. They recognize the leadership characteristics, abilities or potential in others and they assist others, in formal and informal ways, to realize their full potential. They do so in discreet and private ways, as well as publicly recognizable ways. They seek not to have the praise for themselves, as they know their contribution is not possible without the help of others.

GREAT LEADERS DON'T DECIDE EACH DAY TO BE GREAT, THEY JUST ARE

Regardless of where you are at in your leadership journey, whether you think you were born with leadership ability or not, it is vitally important that you feel empowered to exercise all your leadership abilities and not get boxed by yourself or others.

Work on honing those aspects of your character where you feel you can improve. Learn and adapt new ways of doing things. Learn from others, seek feedback and then share what you know works.

The more Great Leaders we have in this world, the better the world will become.

CHAPTER 4
Realizing Your Full Potential

Throughout your life you have received messages like 'Do your best' 'Achieve' 'Realize your potential' but where do you actually learn to do this? There is no formal lesson in how to achieve in life, or to perform at your best. You watch and learn from others. You learn from your own mistakes.

By virtue of your upbringing, your education, your work experience, your experience in relationships, you have acquired many strong skills, knowledge and competencies. Applying these every day and not allowing either a) negative inner thoughts or b) the negative messages from, or controlling and restrictive nature of, others to adversely impact on you, is vital to realizing your full potential.

Why should you not stand proud of your achievements? Why should you be criticized for demonstrating your skills, knowledge and competencies at every opportunity? It's your right, the right of every human, to be given the chance to be who they were born to be.

Each decision that you make, action that you take, word that you speak, breath that you breathe, sets you apart from every other human on this earth.

You are truly unique. There is no-one else like you on this earth. You may have a twin, even an identical twin in appearance, but your soul, your essence, is unique.

You were born for a reason. Find the reason in yourself, nurture and grow the skills, knowledge and competencies that you have, and you will, when the time is right, be who you were born to be.

Your destiny is yours to choose, not another's to dictate. Choose the destiny that resonates well for you. Find calmness and strength within, and you will be empowered to realize that every wish that you have ever made *can* become a reality. Think creative, inspirational and empowering thoughts.

Have patience to know that all the decisions, actions, inactions and errors that you learn from, are for a reason. We fulfil our destinies through all of these things.

Above all, remember that no-one controls you but you — you decide how to react, behave, act, speak etc. There is no ventriloquist behind your back or puppet master above your head.

How many times have you felt that someone is doing just that? Controlling you. It doesn't feel right does it? It feels like their actions are restricting and disempowering you, but what is in fact happening is that you are not taking control for yourself. You are disempowering yourself by allowing others to have influence over you. You and only you decide who will, and to what extent, influence you.

In the first half of 2007 I was faced with a huge personal challenge — whether or not to tell someone I loved at the time, some facts that would rock his very soul. For a long time I thought that to withhold the information would be better, but I knew that time was running out and that each of us deserves to have a full set of facts in order to choose a future path that we believe to be the best. I could see this person on the brink of fulfilling every goal ever set — I shone the light to illuminate truth; I empowered.

I wasn't motivated by personal gain so I empowered at a time when I believed the information would be the most valuable. The shock and subsequent denial of some of the facts presented was pretty significant, but I do know that karmically, I did the right thing. The positive karma that came back to me instantly has shown me I did the right thing.

Sometimes it's difficult and very challenging to make sense of things that are happening every day. When your mind becomes cluttered with useless or too much information it's difficult to see the wood for the trees.

Time is what you must use wisely – to reflect, organize, rearrange or understand. Take time out to clear the debris, the unnecessary memories. Allow your subconscious mind time to process all the data you have inputted each day. Take time to work through your feelings. Listen to your heart. Take time to determine what you really want and then take action.

So many people say to me "My life is so complicated" or "it's complicated". Uncovering truths, exposing lies, re-evaluating decisions, eliminating baggage, gaining a new perspective, setting new goals – all of these things will help to unclutter and simplify your thinking and, in so doing, you will un-complicate and simplify your life.

SIMPLIFY AND UNCLUTTER YOUR MIND TO SIMPLIFY AND UN-COMPLICATE YOUR LIFE

When you have simplified your thinking the answers to realizing your full potential will be right there in front of you. They will illuminate your life as the moon does the sky. They'll bring joy and happiness in a way that you've never experienced. The answers will be lasting, true and sound, for they will have come from within *you* and truly reflect your heart's and soul's desires.

PART 3

Achieving a Lasting and Positive Impact

CHAPTER 1

Eliminating Presentism

So what is presentism?

Is it the opposite of absent? Well no, not exactly.

It's where the *body is present* but the *heart and soul are elsewhere.* The heart and soul are not engaged, not actively in the moment, not 'listening' and being part of where the body is.

Every human has the right to be where they choose to be, at any given point in time. Presentism means that as our body may be present in the *now,* our longing for being in another place is much stronger. We are 'present', but not present at the deepest spiritual and love level in order to give appropriately to those around us. We are holding most of ourselves back.

In every setting and context in life you will see people who are 'present' with their bodies, but their minds, souls and hearts are elsewhere. They make a conscious decision each day to be physically present where they actually don't really want to be. They spend time avoiding the real reason for being there (e.g. socializing rather than actually delivering work; gazing out the window or going outside for a walk instead of participating in a social function; continual inconsistency; using avoidance techniques to keep from doing what they're meant to be doing).

However, once of the worst consequences of presentism in the workplace is when the perpetrator openly admits to being this way and their supervisors do nothing about it.

Many years ago one of my clients was a middle manager level military officer who was promoted to a position involving much people interaction. He worked long hours, felt out of his depth and also felt that his seniors may have doubted their decision to promote him. I showed him, by example, that working long hours did not promote a healthy organizational culture; and encouraged him (against all his training to work 24/7) that people are not machines.

At one stage he suffered an injury which prevented him from writing for several weeks. A few days after the injury I saw him in the corridor. I asked if he was taking things easy and looking out for his wellbeing. He very quickly explained that he was playing the injury for all it was worth to get out of meetings and doing typing etc.

I was rather shocked, but also disappointed by his presentism, particularly given the level he sat in the organization and implicit in that level was to lead by example. In short, an injury is no reason to disengage and suffer presentism, but it was obvious his heart and soul were no longer engaged in what he was doing.

I encouraged him to stay involved by at least attending meetings and listening. He certainly learned fast, but at a critical time, quite unexpectedly, he was transferred to another role. Only the organization knows why they did that but he was quick to see the benefits of the change from a personal perspective. And the person who came in behind him to fill his position? Well, she was given an opportunity to make great change and show what she could do.

When that military officer and I first met I explained to him that he was in the perfect place to make change if he so chose. Many people are placed in organizational positions to learn how to do things better and even to achieve a level of understanding where they may be lacking. Many people also choose positions where they can deliver wonderful outcomes for organizations. The important thing to do, no matter what the reason, is to be fully engaged where you are. Be present and committed. When you feel that ownership and purpose have waned, it's time to leave.

In family settings we see some family members sitting in the same room as each other but their energy is absent; their hearts and souls are elsewhere. They're not engaged. They're not listening, loving, giving and receiving.

Winning hearts and minds and reaching to the soul of others is critical to assisting you to build a bright future for everyone's mutual benefit. The people who share your vision, or whose vision you share, will easily engage with you once clarity is obtained and true purpose is defined. They will exhibit presentism less and less over time.

In the workplace, smart and capable people need to feel they are making a difference or they will leave the organization. This applies to any age or 'generation'. No-one will stick around if they don't feel like they are contributing to something worthwhile, something of goodness, and they certainly won't stay long if they are not valued.

If you know you suffer presentism from time to time, and you don't like it, then work to understand why. Undertake some self-exploration. Work out what your real motivators are, eliminate the barriers to walking forward to the future, understand what you need; and then your heart, mind and soul will be in true synchronicity with your body.

PRESENTISM WON'T SURVIVE WHERE THE HEART, MIND, SOUL AND BODY ARE IN SYNC

CHAPTER 2

Building Successful Business Partnerships

What is the most powerful position in any organization? Is it the Chief Executive Officer? The highest performing sales rep? The Managing Director or Chairman of the Board?

No. It is the receptionist/telephonist. The person who is the voice, the face and/or the ears of the organization every working hour of every working day. Each time the receptionist answers the telephone or greets someone at the front desk the organization is on full show. The receptionist can make or break that first impression, and if the impression they give is negative you've either lost the calling party's interest for good or you're on a difficult path to repairing the damage done.

The number of times you let the phone ring before answering it, your telephone manner, your responsiveness to the caller; whether you delete voice messages without listening to them or not respond to emails – all of these things demonstrate the culture of the organization and your own attitude to people.

In worst case scenarios, some organizations will develop a service charter and then not ensure that it's followed through with. The employees of the organization, each with their own purpose and standards will therefore, through inconsistency, demonstrate there's no corporate standard and ownership of a common set of values.

I've actually heard people, who don't return calls, say "If it's important enough the person will ring back". Would the person have called in the first place if it wasn't important? It's just arrogance to expect someone to chase after you to get a response!

As the leader of an organization you need to set the standard for others to live by. Acknowledge every letter, email and phone call you receive — that is common courtesy. Whilst there are some exceptions, they are very few. If the Queen or Prime Minister has time to respond, then you do too. If you receive an email and it's obvious it requires actioning, then action it. Don't put the topic in the 'too hard' basket. That basket, once created, will never get emptied.

When you work for an organization that has a common set of values and the values are owned by every employee, you can feel it when you walk through the door. That is the hum of the organization — its essence resonating at the correct pitch. The organization will be a winner in every sense of the word. It knows exactly what it wants, expects the same standard from every employee/worker and empowers itself without even having to work hard at it.

As the world grew into the digital and networking age (back in the 1970's and early 80's), it became quite common for multi-national organizations to hold national marketing days — motivational days where they would bring all their employees together to share the vision, the plans, the expected rewards. Companies sometimes called these "Kick-offs". Despite the large expense, what those kinds of exercises do is re-invigorate employees who may have fallen into apathy; they focus everyone on common goals; they articulate the organization's vision in a fun, interactive way; and they engage the hearts, minds and souls of all stakeholders. Done at least once per year, they are a tremendous way to obtain and sustain a corporate edge.

In any type of business partnership - whether it be your team working with another, your Government department providing a service to others, your Branch contract-managing a third party company, your nation trading with another - the parties to that partnership are working for a mutually beneficial outcome. In reality the concept of a WIN/LOSE never enters the equation. There is always a WIN/WIN expectation, otherwise an alliance would not have been formed in the first place, would it?

Strategic planning is a vital component of any business partnership's activities, and the most important aspect of strategic planning is understanding, owning and enunciating what short, medium and long term outcomes are expected. Once all parties know and clearly understand the goals being worked towards, and each understands the part that they play, synchronizing efforts to achieve the outcome(s) become that much easier. A clear and honest intent and vision must be stated up front. The strategic direction must be clearly given, so there is no likelihood for confusion or ambiguity at any stage.

A business partnership can be short term in its efforts but will always be strategic in its outcome impact. The gains, whilst felt in the shorter term, will undoubtedly create an effect at another point in time and it's critical that business partners assess all risks along a time line that stretches far into the future. Every business partnership activity will have a strategic impact whether you pre-define it or not. That is the aspect of power that is least understood.

Every time a 'business' steps forward to make change, a universal energy shift will occur. If the change is a positive one, with honorable outcomes intended, the energy shift will open doors easily and without obstruction. If the change is a negative one with control, greed, deceit, corruption etc. at its core, an energy shift will still occur, but the outcome is controlled more by universal counter-energies than by the partnership seeking the change.

For example, a company has a product to sell. They seek to sell their product to the detriment of other companies — they use subliminal and direct methods to discredit their competitors. You, as the decision maker, can choose to buy the product they're selling, knowing full well that their intent is to achieve a WIN at another's LOSS. The partnership will become awkward as a consequence of its foundation in negative. On the other hand you can acknowledge the company's poor business ethic, decline their offer and then purchase a product from an ethical company that markets itself and its product(s) openly, honestly, and on merit. The second partnership will feel easier, be easier and trust will never be questioned.

The same universal energy principles apply in personal or business relationships. If one person communicating is doing so in a positive way, with honorable outcomes intended, the energy shift will open doors easily and without obstruction. If the communication is a negative one with control, greed, deceit, corruption etc. at its core, an energy shift will still occur but the outcome is controlled more by universal counter-energies than by the person seeking to communicate.

Successful business partnerships require consistent and unwavering devotion to the outcomes being sought, by all parties. They are relationships of interdependency, not co-dependency.

In summary, there are really only a handful of key ingredients in any mutually successful and positively-focused business partnership. In no particular order, they are:

- Respect
- Trust
- Understanding
- Tolerance
- Team Work
- The Willingness to Negotiate to achieve a WIN/WIN Outcome
- A Strategic Focus
- Patience
- Honesty and Integrity
- Flexibility and Adaptability
- Commitment
- Responsiveness.

These values are what underpin an organization and provide the solid foundation for the future.

CHAPTER 3

Using Power Effectively in Command And Control (C2) Organizations

Earlier I gave several examples of behaviors by people trained in military or law enforcement methodologies. Such organizations, quite rightly, require much stricter frameworks, doctrine, values and culture than non-C2 organizations.

In C2 organizations the idea of command can be characterized as *the creative expression of human will necessary to accomplish the mission*[11]. In the same context, control can be characterized as *those structures and processes devised by command to enable it and to manage risk*[12].

Control is thus the indispensable adjunct to the successful expression of command. It provides the means that expedite command as well as the parameters that guide and constrain it. It is the personnel, the facilities and structures, together with the processes for planning, directing and coordinating resources, needed to accomplish the mission.

Because control includes things like standard operating procedures, rules of engagement, regulations, military/specialist law, policies, equipment and other arrangements put in place to facilitate mission success in a safe and efficient manner, it is critical that the personnel in a C2 organization *comply*. They must live and act by the

---

[11] Pigeau R, McCann C. Re-conceptualizing command and control. Canadian Military Journal. Spring 2002:53-63

[12] Ibid

rules or risk punishment — such things as demotion and loss of rank/remuneration; imprisonment for breaching the law; sanctions to ensure modified behaviour, and so on.

Only a particular type of person will choose a career in such a tightly woven organizational structure and rigid culture.

So how do you, as an individual, still express your personality, control your own outcomes and ensure you look out for your team, without being in conflict with the organization?

Let's explore a simple scenario:

You don't agree with what your senior officer has directed you to do. It's placed too great a load on your team of diligent workers. You know you must respect your boss's level/rank at all times so you're loathe to challenge his/her command and direction. How do you speak out without putting your job and career on the line?

Firstly, respecting the 'person' is not a legal requirement in C2 organizations any more than it is in any walk of life. *Respect is something people earn.* (In Part 1, Chapter 3 you learned about positional power and respect, so take some time to reflect on that now before proceeding.)

In some C2 organizations, employees must (by law) respect a higher level/rank no matter what the context. This positional respect provides for and facilitates the chain of command that is so necessary in operational settings. Therefore, it will be far easier to manage interpersonal engagement if you hold respect for your boss as a person, as well as for his/her level/rank.

Before you approach the boss you need to fully understand your motives, the needs of your team, the obstacles to achieving the outcomes expected by your boss, and the unavoidable barriers to producing quality work e.g. limited time, limited support.

As with any communication, starting with a positive is the best way to gain a person's attention. Your tone will be particularly crucial in conveying the importance of what you have to say. Remaining calm, focused, speaking clearly and succinctly and keeping constant eye contact are the four most important ways to project positive energy.

If you falter with what you're saying, if your tone demonstrates doubt or a higher authority than your boss, if you rush what you're saying or lose eye contact, you'll have lost the positive karmic connection.

What if you're hesitating to have eye contact? Are you carrying guilt for something you did to this person and have not corrected; are you feeling insecure; do you lack confidence in what you are saying? There could be any number of reasons and only you will know the answer(s). Eye contact is crucial in initiating, sustaining and growing interpersonal relationships.

Eye contact is not common in C2 organizations. Perhaps this is because the people factor has long been placed second to the 'mission'. Nurturing people and listening to those people working 'below', was not seen to value-add to a strategic outcome, so engagement has fallen by the wayside. It's not a high priority.

Eye contact and being out amongst all staff, working at all levels, 'earths' managers, commanders and senior leaders – they need to be constantly 'earthing' themselves in the reality of their organizations. When we rise up through the hierarchical structure of an organization, it can be very easy to forget what it was like at the bottom. The occasional pull down into the weeds, dealing with issues at the coal face, is essential for senior leaders to regain a full perspective of the organization's culture and tempo.

Only effective C2 organizations realize that their *people are the most important component* in achieving outcomes. Without people to uphold the law, without people to enter countries under threat and assist Governments to restore peace and harmony, without people to transport other people and equipment to overseas destinations, without people willing to risk their lives to save others, C2 organizations would have to close their doors.

People are the most important asset in delivering organizational capability, not the hardware and machines that make up the organization's other resources.

Another power struggle that often appears in C2 organizations is where people at a higher level/rank push hard for their personal agenda to be played out. This is particularly evident when being posted into a position, where you only have a certain amount of time to prove what you can do, thus standing you in better stead for promotion or better opportunities. In this instance, negative personal power is more likely to be used.

You could use level/rank to gain obedience and compliance by your staff, but what is the karmic impact of your actions? Without doubt, a negative one.

For example: You are posted to head up a business unit that needs to deliver a strategic plan affecting the whole organization. You have one year to deliver the product and must, in order for it to be truly effective in the longer term, gain agreement from all stakeholders. You discover along the way that what you're proposing will not be agreed to by everyone so you decide to disengage with the stakeholders and write the plan in isolation. The governing committee, responsible for endorsing the plan and agreeing to resources for its implementation, are so tied down with other priorities they don't ask for validation of the methodology and therefore agree to the plan not realizing it's not fully supported by those who will be required to implement it.

You've achieved your goal, but what's the cost to the organization and its people? Do you really care, or is it just the promotion that's the motivator?

Using your personal power in ways that focuses on benefits for the majority is far more constructive and positive than simply getting the job done and ticking that box at promotion hearing time.

Further, whilst ever we have C2 organizations managing critical work, the organizational culture must also sustain a strategic risk management focus — a very long term (50+ year) focus - where risk management is the principal governance tool.

Each activity in and outcome for an organization forms the whole. Each individual's actions and words will have a strategic impact on the organization and its future health.

What leaders in C2 organizations must learn to do is actively listen to their people, refresh their approach to outputs and outcomes and how they are to be achieved, learn from mistakes and actually *apply* the learnings, and finally, seek change when old ways prove to be toxic and stagnating.

The challenge for C2 organizations lies in teaching its employees how to use their personal power constructively when *not* engaged with the enemy or in high risk settings. For military personnel, for instance, given that a new recruit will be trained to fight in the face of eminent death (and override any natural instinct to flee), and that they must stand ready to engage with an 'enemy' at every turn, it's crucial that recruits are also trained how to *disengage from the war-fighting mode* when their workplace isn't the battlefield.

Those working inside C2 organizations are often seen as using a directive, imposing, paternalistic and non-compromising tone with others, even with their own families. This isn't an effective use of personal power and the onus lies predominantly with the organization to teach its employees how to switch *off* the C2 mode of communication when that's not required. Family relationships will survive and thrive longer when this is done.

It's also crucial for the long term wellbeing of the employee, as they leave the organization, to be re-programmed to a more positive, constructive and nurturing way of communicating so that strategic harm isn't done to future generations.

C2 organizations must recognize they have an obligation that extends far beyond just meeting their operational missions. They have an ongoing obligation to ensure the restoration of normality for individuals, families and communities. This will assist individuals and families to relax, decompress and gain normality (in societal terms) after the C2 activities are no longer part of life.

All too often (and with increasing regularity in this 21st century) we hear of men and women, torn by guilt or shame over the activities they have undertaken for their C2 organization, take their own lives, commit an act of terror or violence in their community, or sink into the darkness of alcoholism, other drug dependency, or domestic violence. These symptoms speak loudly of the obligations of all (the individual, their families, and their employer) to make situations right again.

Without that restoration of good karma, bringing 'good' back to a bad situation, the karmic implications will be grave.

No Boxing Allowed

CHAPTER 4
Enriching Personal Relationships

One of the most challenging things we humans face each day is understanding each other. We're not able to read minds, so ultimately we must learn and trust the motivations, actions, words and interests of others as they're displayed each day.

As you would well know, that's a pretty tough ask for many folk.

When disappointment clouds our judgment, when fear stifles our trust, when another's errors and bad behavior cause us to question our loyalty, we humans have to work doubly hard to discern truth and find what's fair and just to do or say.

The balancing of each other's needs and the juggling of relationship dynamics day-to-day are, by far, the hardest set of skills any human will have to learn. And, of course, some will be hopeless at it; some will be great; and many will be somewhere in the middle, floundering about repeating mistakes and not learning lessons quickly enough.

Since the age of seven I have been observing people, in every context and stage of my life. To the most part, despite some horrific incidents that could have flattened me, I've enjoyed observing them. I learn so much when I watch and listen to people.

At the age of 50, as my head started to fill with the words that have subsequently filled these pages, I started writing this book. In delivering *No Boxing Allowed* then, and refreshing it now in 2016 (to ensure that every message is as clear as I can make it), it gave me the opportunity to share all that I had learned through a long professional career that most would die for, and from my personal life experiences, many of which most would shy away living through.

I always reflect – on my actions and words, those of others, and also on what *didn't* happen. The "hindsight is 20/20" vision rule really does apply. Having courage to face the lessons is another thing, as you would realize.

What I have managed to cement an understanding of, is that there are only a few truly valuable foundation stones needed for peaceful, loving and enriched personal relationships with others. Those listed in the last Chapter 2, and:

- empower people with information
- respect each other's personal space
- heal yourself from pain of the past and don't force others to live with your pain
- support others to heal
- share experiences and learnings as widely as possible so that mistakes are not repeated through generations
- understand what went wrong; learn from the experience
- actively listen
- change your dialogue to the positive – eliminate "try", "trying" and "can't" from your vocabulary and substitute empowering confidence-based words and phrases like "doing my best to", "currently working to", "are", "will" etc.
- love unconditionally
- forgive.

In any personal relationship there are times when we feel like pushing for something to change. The negative energy created when you push too hard for something to change or happen though, will actually work against you in resolving the challenge.

A simple example of this is where a husband and wife constantly argue about where to reside. One wants to sell and move, another wants to stay in the home. Whilst ever there is a difference in motivation and yearning the outcome won't be achieved. One will always feel they are getting the raw end of the deal, that they're not getting what they need. But, when the pressure is taken off, time passes and perspectives change, a compromise and **WIN/WIN** is then more likely to occur.

By far the best and most positive long-term solution to any difference of opinion is to allow time to pass, needs or wants to change and pain to be healed.

A WIN/WIN outcome is the best solution. Compromise by one or both parties, whilst difficult or challenging at first, may just be the pivot for the change required. I'm not suggesting that you back down and don't hold to your convictions. It's essential you maintain your standards at all times. What you do need to do is work to understand the other person's perspective, compare it to your own, check the differences and come up with a strategy that accommodates the needs and wants of both, as much as possible. Perhaps one person will miss out on some aspect, but as long as the majority outcome for both is achieved you'll have a WIN/WIN to celebrate.

When humans push really hard for change, or engage with others in a confrontational manner, the negative energy created will always work *against* finding the best solution. The more you push for an outcome that is only for your own good, and not mutually beneficial, the more resistance you'll strike from others. The instant you stop pushing for an outcome that you believe is the only valid outcome, universal energy will shift in the opposite direction, pressure will come off without you even knowing, and the best solution will surface very soon thereafter.

The key point I'm making here is the *best* solution. You can push hard all you like, not give an inch and make *something* happen just for the sake of it, but the long term outcome will never be the best one.

THE INSTANT YOU STOP 'PUSHING' THE BEST SOLUTION WILL COME

I've thought long and hard about the two most important improvements we humans can make to our existence; what will create strategic benefits for millennia to come.

These are your two challenges:

1. The Celebration of Life

Many people say they don't celebrate birthdays. Are someone's life and their entry into this world not worth celebrating each anniversary? We celebrate wedding anniversaries, Christmas, Easter, national holidays and the ending of wars but not a loved one's or our own birthday. Why is the celebration of events that relate to those who have died more important than those who are living? Is our importance to the world greater once we die?

I therefore suggest that to show appreciation for your own life and the life of others you hold dear by acknowledging birthdays, is the simplest, easiest and most positively validating gesture of personal power you can ever give.

2. Allowing Men to Cry

How often have you heard men say to other men or boys "Don't be a girl", "Only a sissy cries" or "Wipe your eyes princess". Why should men not be allowed to express their feelings? Men cry when they are in pain too. That's a positive and motivating thing to do.

Just imagine all the men in the world crying long enough and often enough to release their pain. We'd see a major reduction in the number of fights, arguments, wars and atrocities being acted out each day. A man's anger, when misdirected or bottled up, is a major destructive force. So too is a woman's, but her natural instinct (and to a certain extent societal expectation) is to cry to release tension and pain.

As a member of the human race each of us needs to work diligently and consistently to encourage men to release their pain. That will place us one giant step closer to universal peace.

CHAPTER 5
Priceless Gifts

I trust that you've journeyed well through *No Boxing Allowed*. You've learned many things in your life thus far and your learnings will continue as long as your soul needs the lessons.

The human race in its entirety has been very slow in growing to a decent level of emotional maturity. We're a highly intelligent species, have huge capacity to make change, and have enormous potential to do great things, but at times we display behaviors that remind us just how far our journey is yet to be.

Self-realization is an important aspect of a human's evolution and is a critical part of your soul's journey to maturity. Through reading this book and applying its teachings you will, if not already, achieve self-realization and improved Self-Intelligence — knowing yourself fully and completely and how to channel your endless positive power in the right ways.

And it's when you've reached that point that you'll be able to know and help others.

I encourage you to realize and learn from what's happening all around you, all the time. Recognize and accept that forces are working for and sometimes against you — forces that you're not able to control, triggering decisions of and actions by others. Knowing and accepting that you don't have control over anything or anyone but yourself will assist you to find inner harmony and serenity.

Channelling your inner power appropriately and positively is a priceless gift that you give, every day, to the world around you. And as you learn more about your and others' personal power you'll see there are many priceless gifts in life. They don't have a price tag and you're not able to go to the store and buy them. They're all around you, every day.

The bird that rests on the line and gives you eye contact as you hang out the washing, the stranger who nods and smiles at you as they pass, the child who hugs you without uttering a sound, the hand that touches your arm in sympathy, the long loving look given by another, the hand that holds yours tenderly and softly, the teenager who strives to be just like you, the baby who beams when they see you, the colleague who gives you support to achieve your goals, the comforting touch of a friend when they know you're struggling, the bunch of flowers or card that says "thank you", the positive karma you receive from others every day — they are all priceless gifts.

Never take them for granted.

Remember too that no-one has the monopoly on knowledge and experience; we all learn from each other. And there are no failures in life, only opportunities from which to learn and grow.

THERE ARE NO FAILURES IN LIFE, ONLY OPPORTUNITIES FROM WHICH TO LEARN AND GROW

It's by sharing information and being the best we can be that we become most powerful. Your one voice can make or break a situation. Your one heart and how you express it can crush or nurture another human being.

It's vital that you don't punish others for their inadequacies, fears and any injustice to you. Let karma return to those who do wrong by you, in its own time. Have faith and trust that universal justice will be served. You don't need to be a party to the karmic lessons of others — they'll happen anyway, without your intervention.

As we put out goodness, so it will come to us. As we express gratitude for life's blessings and gifts, and give to the world and others, so will the world continue to give in ways we never expected.

The minute we stop giving, we fall back to selfishness and cruelty. Nothing good grows out of selfish and cruelty, just chronic pain and dysfunction.

True wisdom comes when we know that:

- we humans do not hold all the answers,
- material wealth and possessions are not the measure of success nor do they bring happiness and fulfilment,
- no human being is perfect;

and, when we:

- find the capacity to forgive ourselves, not just others, and
- continually reach out for more lessons to apply.

**When you know you've found
your inner peace,
share that priceless gift of serenity
with others.

The world will be a better place
for the goodness that you bring.**

www.ingramcontent.com/pod-product-compliance
Lightning Source LLC
Chambersburg PA
CBHW050556300426
44112CB00013B/1950